SOFT SELLING
IN A
HARD WORLD

PLAIN TALK ON THE
ART OF PERSUASION

BY JERRY VASS

RUNNING PRESS
PHILADELPHIA • LONDON

Second Edition

9 8 7 6 5 4 3 2 1
Digit on the right indicates the number of this printing

Library of Congress Cataloging-in-Publication Number 98-65178

ISBN 0-7624-0401-9

Cover design by Toni Leslie
Edited by Greg Jones

This book may be orderd by mail from the publisher.
Please include $2.50 for postage and handling.
But try your bookstore first!

Running Press Book Publishers
125 South Twenty-second Street
Philadelphia, Pennsylvania 19103-4399

Contents

PART II
BUILDING YOUR PRESENTATION

PART III
SURVIVAL SKILLS FOR THE STREET SOLDIER

PART IV
BUILDING YOUR SELLING PLAYBOOK

Preface

People waste their lives trying to sell. They get confused between persuasion as a belief system ("You have to believe in what you sell.") and persuasion as a natural talent ("You can't teach anyone how to sell."). SOFT SELLING IN A HARD WORLD™ is designed to clear up that confusion.

If you aren't selling up to your potential, you probably don't understand that selling is a game. Most people don't. Those who *do* make 85% of the money, become executives, or run their own successful businesses. This book is about that game—how to play it, when to play it, where to play it, and with whom.

This book is about fulfilling your potential without resorting to "motivational" and "inspirational" beliefs. As in sports, you'll find that certain mechanical moves need to be mastered before your inspiration or genius can shine. A dog can become inspired to chase a car but doesn't know what to do with the car once it's caught it. This knowledge is about what you do when you catch the car, that thin slice of face-to-face time with the Buyer when persuasion actually occurs.

This is a handbook. There is very little theory—it is nearly all mechanics. While there is a certain primitive logic in the way this story is told, you can begin to read on any page and profit.

This is a perfect book for the bathroom. Studied and practiced in small bites over time, the culturally awkward acts required to persuade others will become automatic. The selling trade takes practice. Everything worthwhile does. Sex and selling are the only endeavors that the human being is expected to perform perfectly the first time without practice. By now, you know the fallacy of the first illusion. The second illusion is even more embarrassing.

Read gently. Enjoy your profession, for the selling profession is really about making more trusting friends than you ever thought possible.

THANKS

A heartfelt thanks to my loyal clients. They paid me well and kept me alive long enough to learn the stuff I pass on to you. Their high expectations and uncompromising performance standards made me good.

And thanks to the brightest people in the country, those super-salespeople, the front-line street-soldiers who were my students through the years. This book is for them. They taught me how to sell. They made me laugh.

J.V.

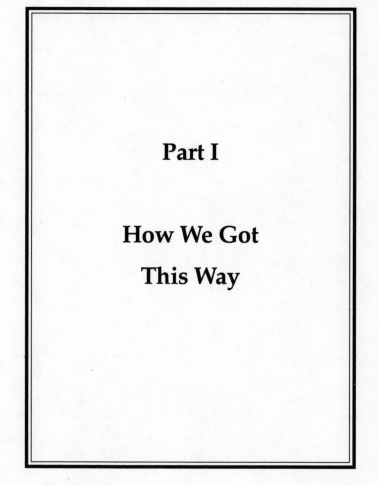

Part I

How We Got
This Way

HOW TO GET RICH QUICK!

It's just around the corner . . .

There are few legal ways to get rich quick. Your chance of finding one is approximately one in 2 million . . . or about twice the odds of getting hurt in a commercial plane crash. Now, the bright side. Getting rich slowly is fun, too, yielding thousands of little adventures along the way. Hot pursuit of the almighty buck is the American way. Yet, when the pursuit is over, it's hard to remember exactly how you made the big money or where it went. But you'll always remember your great selling presentations.

There are only three ways to make exceptional money:

- To work in a place nobody wants to be

- To perform work nobody else wants to do

- To perform work nobody else can do

It's the last two conditions for making extraordinary money that we will explore here.

Learning to sell softly isn't only about money—it's about enjoying life's working trip. This little manual is about reality. It's a survival guide for the strange, hilly country of persuasion. It shows you how to work less, enjoy more, and have a great journey. Its goal: to destroy selling illusions and replace them with selling tools that work.

Unless carefully trained, ordinary salespeople use their egos to sell; their egos appear at the wrong time, at the wrong place, and for the wrong reason. That's why ordinary salespeople don't make much money, and Buyers shut them down without mercy.

Soft Selling in a Hard World™ is about redesigning how we sell. This redesign has proven to be exceedingly effective for salespeople of every experience level— from high school kids selling magazine subscriptions to chairmen of the board selling mergers and acquisitions.

This book is about mechanics. It is designed from the street up—tactics, not strategy. You won't find magic here; there is none. Nor will you need a Kierkegaardian leap of faith. There is no underlying motivation or belief system. It isn't about something larger than yourself. You don't have to believe in it to make it pay. You don't even have to believe in yourself. You just have to use the mechanics.

You *will* find Soft Selling in a Hard World™ exciting because nothing motivates like unbridled success—the success of persuading people to do what you would like them to do.

HOW SELLING GOT TACKY

It's a dirty game . . .

Selling is the highest paid profession in the world. Our leaders in business, politics, research, and the arts are all great salespeople or they have great salespeople on their payrolls. In our culture, skillful persuasion is an integral part of any successful endeavor. At some critical point in their careers these leaders needed to sell their ideas. Doing so turned the corner for them and carried them above their competitors.

Even if you have a world class idea and want to give it away for the good of humanity, you will have to sell the concept. If you can't sell it, you'll be stuck with your idea, poorer for your brilliance and generosity. It seems unfair but even freebies must be delivered with a certain salesmanship or the receiver does not perceive the true value of the gift.

Everything has to be sold. Yet so few people sell well that 15% of them make 85% of the available money. At your next sales meeting with 20 people, three will take home the money of 17 others. What is it that allows these three people to have all that money flow their way? Is it luck, hard work, and a good attitude? Or is it persuasive skill—understanding the transactional dynamics of the selling process? After teaching sales for 20 years, I have found that the people who succeed consistently are skillful in verbal communication and understand the game dynamics of the transaction.

As a child, you are taught a popular illusion by anxious parents and tenured professors—if you learn a profession well and work hard, your future is secure and you will inevitably rise to the top, drive a fast car, and find beautiful people of the opposite sex pursuing you relentlessly. Like so many romantic promises, this is only an illusion. What parents and professors don't tell you is that the closer you get to the top, the better you must know how to sell because everyone at the top sells better. If you are going to the top of your profession, you must sell well, too.

I have a friend who is the president and chairman of the board of a large banking institution in the Northeast. Historically, bankers are the third worst salespeople in the world. (MBAs are first and engineers are second.) One evening over beers, I asked him how he perceived his job. "I am a salesman," he said. "I have to sell policy changes and new ideas. I sell the board of directors, the stockholders, the branch managers, the tellers, the cleaning crew, and the customers all at the same time." Incidentally, this salesman's salary is well over a million a year. Does he know something about banking? "Yes," he says with a big grin, ". . . but there are many people who know more about banking."

So you need two professions: the one you have studied all this time, and your "other profession"—the profession of persuasion that allows you to make good use of all those years of education, practice, and dues-paying.

Obviously, it is important to learn and refine the skills of your chosen profession. Unfortunately, many of these skills will go wasted if you cannot get others to see and use the benefits of your knowledge.

Certain perverse people believe selling should be fun. I am one of them. Inside most firms and institutions selling is looked upon as a dirty but necessary business, tainting all those designated by bad luck or low station to pursue it; a demeaning job to be handed off to someone else as soon as you are kicked upstairs.

Horror stories of the unwilling and unprepared salesperson who is trapped in a presentation and must perform or lose the farm is grist for the humor writer's mill. Since sales is a game like any other sport, these poor folks lose at a game they do not realize is being played.

Life is not designed to be a miserable existence; it is designed to be enjoyed. The enjoyment includes work and especially persuasion. Selling is fun when you learn the game. Persuading other people to do what you want is a terrific sport. You don't believe it? The folks who sell well are having a wonderful time. Whether they were good at sales first or had fun first is unclear. But the message is clear—selling well means laughing a lot.

The seriousness with which management, sales managers, and motivational speakers address this most joyful of trades is depressing. The promise of a good time after becoming successful is not nearly as much fun as having a good time while getting there. Like life, it isn't the destination, it's the journey that counts.

In our culture, salespeople have a dubious image—lazy, disorganized, uncontrollable, unaccountable, unable to hold a regular job. If you can't do anything else, you can always be a salesperson.

Just the opposite is true. The best salespeople are so good (and often so far up the ladder) they don't appear to sell.

The selling profession has at least a five-year apprenticeship under good management. The best salespeople are trustworthy to a fault, conscientious, and hardworking. They make money the old-fashioned way: they earn it.

Ordinary people sell poorly because they don't understand that sales is a technical transaction. Good talkers often choose to become sales professionals. Unfortunately, they confuse talk with persuasion; they don't understand that selling well means listening well. Selling is problem solving, not hustling. Aggressiveness propels you into the mean streets but ruins sales.

Most salespeople won't stop talking long enough to let the Buyer make a decision. They fear the silence required for the Buyer to think. They guess at the Buyer's needs, and guess and guess and guess. And they are nearly always wrong. They work as if the Buyer cared about establishing a long term relationship with the Seller. To compound the error, they attempt to direct the Buyer into a decision using cheap semantic tricks taught to them by pots-and-pans salesmen.

Because Sellers are so often rebuffed or ignored by Buyers, the salesperson feels that selling is warfare: the Buyer is the enemy and words are ammunition. The Buyer knows the selling tricks and feels he is simply a mark for the Seller's commission check. The Buyer's defenses go on full alert. The Seller's advances are turned aside because they are so predictable, amateurish, and easily deflected.

Since the Buyer has so much more resistance than the Seller has stamina, the Seller runs out of courage, becomes listless and loses more often. And then the downward spiral begins. It's burnout time. A job change is in the wind. Again. Salespeople are cannon-fodder for the capitalistic warfare between Buyer and Seller.

The single reason for a salesperson's existence is to get the Buyer's commitment. Just how poor are salespeople at their jobs? In a study of professional salespeople (those who sell full time), 50% failed to ask for the Buyer's commitment to buy. This low level of performance is a waste of their company's money and a waste of everyone's time.

Our culture has repressed our listening skills. The media background noise, movies, TV, radio and print advertising all cater to that passive part of our mind that slows down for entertainment. In the ceaseless search for entertainment, we have lost the skills to listen critically to our conversational partner. We no longer actively listen to stories as we did before electronics. We passively watch them artificially reproduced as abstractly polished images moving in the two dimensions of the projection screen rather than the three dimensions of our minds. Whole lives are portrayed in two fast-paced, glitzy hours. We don't listen to what people say even when our livelihood depends on it. We have become a nation of 260-million talking heads.

Studies show that the higher in business people get, the more information they obtain by listening. In tests at the boardroom level, executives retained 90% of the information delivered in a 45-minute presentation. Assembly line workers retained 25%. Which came first: listening skills or promotion? Who knows? For the average person, improving listening skills is a reasonable ambition. You may never make the boardroom, but it may get you off the assembly line.

Since birth we have been told the cultural fairy tale about the "born salesman." Many people who say "I can't sell a thing" compare themselves with these few shining lights. There are exactly as many born salespeople as there are born neurosurgeons, about 2% of the total. The rest of us must learn the selling profession.

Formal schooling doesn't offer degrees in sales. There are degrees in marketing but none in persuasion. Usually persuasion is learned on the street or from veterans who took their hits on the sidewalks. Be at ease, my selling friend; good salespeople got good by getting killed, learning why they died, and then vowing never to die exactly the same way ever again.

3

WHY THE *SOFT SELL* WORKS

Living well is the best revenge . . .

The "hard sell" approach has developed as a natural outgrowth of the American culture. It sounds normal to us as Buyers because our defensive agents are calloused to the constant attack of hard-sell messages. While defending ourselves against attack and sorting the puffery from representation, we make mincemeat of the salesperson. The hard sell doesn't work well anymore. Buyers are hardened to attacks on their common sense.

Even though Buyers may not like the hard sell, they accept or reject it with a certain practiced comfort. They have heard it all before and their minds are prepared to deal with it. They listen and look for anything that triggers their defensive mechanisms—wrong tone of voice, negative body language, doubtful words—any attack, direct or implied. When their defensive agents spot something aggressive, Buyers reflexively erect armor against the Seller.

However, when the mechanics of the sales presentation are changed to deliver messages to the Buyer that bypass the usual attack routes, they flank the defensive armor. It is possible to have Buyers commit to a purchase rather painlessly, sometimes without even knowing it. Even when Buyers realize they are being persuaded, they still enjoy it. Their "soldiers" are not prepared to mount a defense to say no—they just stand around and watch.

When you learn to sell softly, you retrain the old hard-sell habits you've built up over years of living in our culture. In learning the *Soft Sell*, first you learn new moves, how they are constructed and when to use them based on the Buyer's usual hard-sell responses. Then, you practice to get your new habits in place. Once in place, your new habits do the selling work for you almost effortlessly.

It is much easier to teach soft selling techniques to new salespeople than to experienced, "high-mileage" salespeople. The new kids don't have all those hard-sell habits getting in their way. High-mileage salespeople are a seething mass of illusion, bad information, enculturation, poor role models, flaky images, and hardened habits. They confuse motivation with sales training. They feel that they are so good and so experienced they don't need to practice. Their hard-sell agents tell them that really good salespeople don't need to study the profession of persuasion, which is like saying the quarterback for the Super Bowl team doesn't need to practice and should only play during the game itself.

4.

WHAT IS A SALESPERSON?

If you can't get a regular job . . .

My young daughter asked me for career advice. I told her, "Go into sales. Pick a profession that feels that selling is a sleazy activity, below its professional standards. Study that profession with the idea that you'll make your money selling. There will be little competition and your colleagues will be delighted to pay you handsomely, even more than they earn themselves."

When asked what they really do, most top executives admit, "I sell." During selling courses, they often make the most convincing presentations. Of course, occasionally, they make the worst presentations.

Sales is a profession identified with the worst of its practitioners, not the best. Because they sell so well, the public doesn't identify those at the top of the cultural heap—the politicians, movie stars, talk-show hosts, televangelists, and business leaders—as salespeople. As outstanding salespeople, they are rarely caught practicing the selling trade.

The best of them are so good that people simply like their "personalities." People easily confuse skill with personality. When you study the best, you find they

You need two professions: Your profession and the "other profession," the profession of persuasion.

make many mechanical selling moves exactly right. Is this due to practice or coincidence? Natural talent or learned response? Only they know for sure how much is talent and how much is learned. The results are the same. They convince, move ideas, create change, and solve problems. We love them for it and reward them with the best our culture offers: fame, fortune, cool clothes, and big houses.

5.

THE CULTURAL CONTRACT

Made to be broken . . .

Except for some cultural snobs, every home has at least one television and several radios. Cable and satellite TV surround us. Billboards, newspapers, magazines, internet, direct mail, even clothes attack us.

The advertising industry reports that the city person is bombarded by 61,000 advertising messages every day. Us consumers handle the overload by not handling it at all. Targeted by this media assault, they tune out civilization. They refuse to carry the load because they can't carry it and stay sane. Besides, who cares about all that drivel?

The industrial revolution and mass production brought mass selling. Until then, selling was personal: food-stuffs, handicrafts, tradesmen's services, livestock, etc. Goods and services were sold by the producer directly to the user. When mass production grew it predictably overloaded inventories and someone was hired to sell the overstock. Voila!—a new profession was born.

That new pox upon the land, mass merchandising, erupted with newspapers and radio. The television huckster—strident, price-conscious, aggressive, and abrasive—embodied the new image of the salesperson and replaced the wagon-bed snake-oil salesman and the side show barker.

As children, the cultural stereotype of the American salesperson became part of our lives. We watched continuous commercials interrupted every few minutes by Road Runner and Bugs Bunny. Even the pre-TV Bugs adopted his unique brand of urbane shyster slickness from real hustlers. Later, he was perfectly copied by real-life TV hucksters, completing the circle. The selling stereotype became ingrained in us.

When we find ourselves selling, the image of the TV pitchman is our subconscious role model. As the stereotype, we envision ourselves pitching to a willing, watching audience, mesmerizing them with the power of our golden words—like a rock star.

As Buyers, we endure pitching; we ignore unprovable claims; we suffer abrasiveness. We know it's just the selling game, but we distrust salespeople who work like this. They don't get to us very often. When they do, it's usually an unhappy experience, leaving us with the vague feeling that somehow we lost and they won. A classic zero-sum game—the Seller wins, the Buyer loses.

The best salespeople are so good, they don't appear to be selling.

We are so convinced that sales is pitching, we accept low levels of sales success and think nothing of it. Put on your selling hat and your personality changes. Suddenly you are the goal-striver, the attacker, the shuck-and-jive pitchman of your business. Glossy words and a forceful stance in thought and deed become your stock-in-trade. The exhortations of the sales manager, the motivational speaker, or your own rampant ambition must be heeded. Still, you hate the feeling. Even winning doesn't feel as rewarding as it should. Why do you feel like you are losing? Is it a double bind—the Buyer and the Seller both lose? Is it selling warfare?

Those reactions are cultural. In our cultural agreement, "The Seller attacks—the Buyer defends." As Buyers, our emotions are armor-plated just like a medieval knight. We see and hear little. We are totally self-involved. The defending armor is built to protect against unskilled, aggressive salespeople hammering at us . . . beating us until we are numb. The Buyer's armor is a mind-callous developed from rough handling. For salespeople, that's bad news.

But there is good news: the armor covers only the front of the Buyer. Behind, their unprotected bums flap in the open breeze, willing and waiting to be seen by anyone who shows enough sense and technical selling skill to get behind their frontal armor. Why no armor-plate back there? Because salespeople skillful enough to get behind the Buyers' armor treat them gently, tactfully, and respectfully so there is no ugly armor buildup. The Buyers find no need to defend themselves. This technique of flanking the Buyer's armor is called the *Soft Sell*.

6.

WHAT DO YOU SELL FIRST?

Illusion to the death . . .

About the only thing ordinary salespeople agree upon is the idea that you must sell yourself first. This notion seems to have universal acceptance.

Here is a short drill. Do this drill. Don't skip over it searching for some career-altering magic bullet later on in the book. It is a short and relatively painless exercise.

Here's the scene: You just received a call from a lawyer representing your Uncle Willy. Your uncle became estranged from the family when you were a child, moved to the West, and got rich in the junk business. He's just passed on to the great junkyard in the sky. Since he smelled bad, never got on well with the ladies, and never produced heirs, you are named in his will.

His lawyer tells you that you have been left a legacy. ("Oh, boy," you think, "here's the new BMW I've been lusting after.") The lawyer goes on: Uncle Willy knew you were in sales and, in the spirit of America, left you the greatest gift he knew—the gift of opportunity.

So instead of leaving you a pile of cash, Uncle Willy bought you a 60-second TV commercial on the most popular late night talk show. You don't get any money but you do get the opportunity to stand up and sell yourself to thirty-million people watching you between their toes.

Write a one-minute television spot selling yourself. It should run about 120 words long—about one page of double-spaced typewritten copy. (This is perhaps the most valuable lesson in this book so don't turn to the next page until this assignment is done. Remember, trustworthiness is a trait of the superior salesperson. Also, don't cop out. Don't let a little thing like having to write one page of copy delay your success.)

Write your 60-second commercial here (or use a separate sheet of paper):

Now look critically at what you have written. Answer the following questions:

1. Taking the global view, that is, compared to other people in the world, would you buy from this person?

2. Since the only reason for being a salesperson is to get a commitment from the Buyer, did you ask for a commitment? Circle your closing statement or question asking for the Buyer's commitment.

3. What was the most used word in the commercial? Circle every "I" in the script.

Here are the typical responses from students in VASS® EXECUTIVE SALES TRAINING workshops:

1. Without any warning, I ask students to give their presentations verbally; most are poorly thought out. You would think that after two or three weak commercials, everyone else would frantically prepare. They don't. They wait for the train to run over them. It seems a simple exercise. It isn't. While salespeople agree that they must sell themselves first, it is an unusual case, even remarkable, when they actually know how to do so.

2. Getting the order is the raison d'etre for the sales-person. Out of a hundred students, only four or five

will ask the Buyer to take any action toward commitment, even to calling an imaginary toll-free
telephone number.

3. The most used word: "I."

The obvious question arising from this exercise: If you
believe you sell yourself first, why aren't you better
prepared to do so?

You have believed this illusion without questioning the
validity of the idea. Tell a lie often enough and everyone will believe it. You've heard that before. Here it is
in living color. To most of us, "selling yourself" means
being friendly or professional or technically competent
or having a dynamic personality. Maybe a great smile
or dressing correctly or marrying the boss's favorite
offspring helps.

The reality is that selling yourself is a technical exercise
requiring transactional mechanics. Properly done, your
personality, smile, connections, and technical knowledge become secondary issues.

If half of the professional salespeople in America never
ask for the order, the remaining half usually ask for the
order crudely and abrasively, attacking the Buyer at the
pivotal moment of seduction. In spite of this childlike

awkwardness, those who ask for the order most often close the most sales.

A sale is closed the moment the Buyer's mind agrees with your presentation. What you, the Seller, are looking for is Buyer commitment. If you aren't looking for the Buyer's commitment, then you are a professional guest, a hanger-on in the business world, a nonproductive sycophant searching perpetually for the free gift of business from a merciful Buyer. Good luck! You'll need it.

About the word "I." If you learn nothing else from this little book, learn this well: When you are selling, nobody cares whether you live or die as long as you don't die on their property. The Buyer prefers that you die on government property where someone will take care of your untidy remains.

Let's examine this for a moment. Who is the Buyer worried about most? Who concerns the Buyer day and night? Whose pocketbook and prestige are at stake? Whose career is most important? Who is the Buyer thinking about while talking to you?

The Buyer's single, ongoing, residual concern in the entire world is that individual's own interest. Just like you. Buyers aren't "them." Buyers are "us."

The Buyer has three questions: "So what?", "What's in it for me?", and "Can you prove it?"

As Buyers, we don't give a skinny rat's behind about salespeople, only about the benefits they offer "us." So here is the rule: The word "I" has no place in a sales presentation.

At best, "selling yourself first" is a shaky idea on which to base a profession: it is a myth. You do not sell yourself first. In real life, you sell Buyers the benefits of your solution to their business and personal problems.

So, on the premise that Buyers are us, let's discuss how we got to be the way we are.

And about your commercial—even great execution cannot save a poor concept. Even when attempting to sell yourself, you must put your ego away and sell the benefits you bring to the Buyer.

Return to your 60-second commercial and underline the Benefits you wrote for the Buyer.

7.

THE "I" CHART

Stealing back the spotlight . . .

The ordinary presentation includes innumerable references back to the salesperson. Usually "I" is used. We more sensitive types substitute "we."

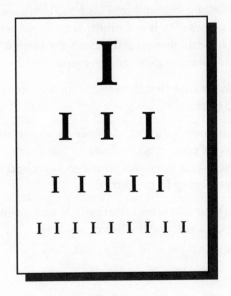

The Salesperson's I Chart

Stay off the I Chart. Eliminating I from your selling presentation increases your sales.

Sprinkling "I" throughout the presentation like raisins in oatmeal constantly shifts the emphasis away from the Buyer back toward the Seller. The phrase, "I think . . ." is most common.

Here are three reasons not to use "I think . . .":

1. Redundancy. If you say it, you must think it.

2. Professionals don't think; professionals know.

3. Pulls the center of attention toward you rather than the Buyer.

Since the Buyer's whole being is self-seeking, stating what you think weakens your presentation and easily raises arguments in the Buyer's mind. Even when the Buyer asks, "What do you think?" they really mean, "What do you know?"

"I think . . ." is deeply buried in our everyday usage. It's a habit you probably own and just never noticed. Start noticing it now. During my selling courses, each time someone uses that self-serving qualifier, everyone in class snaps their fingers. Within two hours all students begin to alter their behavior away from themselves and closer to the Buyer's point-of-view, putting their own opinions aside in an attempt to find the Buyer's.

When you're selling, nobody cares what you think.

According to a Yale University study, the twelve most persuasive words in the language are:

- you
- money
- save
- new
- results
- easy
- health
- safety
- love
- discovery
- proven
- guarantee

Proctor and Gamble, who spends billions on advertising added "free" and "sex" to the list.

You will notice the word "I" appears neither in this list nor will it appear in a list a hundred times as long.

8

PUFFERY AND REPRESENTATION

The expensive warm wind . . .

Puffery is hot air. Webster's Dictionary defines it as,
"Flattering publicity, exaggerated commendation
especially for promotional purposes." In selling, it is
claims that are unproven as stated. Some typical puffery
words and phrases:

- "We're Number One . . ."
- "We're the best in our business (city/region/
  nation/galaxy) . . ."
- . . . save big money
- . . . a lot
- . . . high profits
- . . . the fastest, etc.

While these examples of puffery are stock-in-trade for
the advertising business, as a Buyer you don't take
them seriously. No one else does either. As Sellers, we
want to be taken seriously by everyone we meet. We
have tons of money involved, oft times survival itself.
The fastest way to break trust with your Buyer is to
waggle your verbal finger high in the air and claim that
you or your company is "Number One."

Representation, on the other hand, is provable, defendable, and believable. Webster's defines it as, "Statement of fact."

Representations are facts proven as stated—figures, testimonials, expert opinions, published articles, or any other hard information about the product or service from a reputable source.

Some typical representational statements:

- Increase profits by 8%
- Cut labor costs by 4%
- Save 45 minutes per day
- In the same location since 1970

In sales, puffery is a way of life. The Buyer's armor-plated defenses expect puffery. The Buyer is rarely disappointed. The Buyer also expects to distrust you or what you say. (You know how salespeople lie.) With much justification, the Buyer shrugs you off. This is a significant reason salespeople are perceived as bothersome clones. Most of us make the same mistakes and use the same words; we sound interchangeable. We sound like a poorly conceived TV commercial.

Salespeople use puffery—words like "the best" or "fastest" or "Number One." Nobody believes them.

Puff statements:

"Because we have been in business for so long, you can rely on us to be there when you need us."

"As you may know, we are Number One in the market."

There are other puff words that, like a black hole in the universe, absorb more energy than they transmit. Like any new trend, these energy absorbers develop currency and become fashionable. People use them to make themselves sound important as full service, proactive, professional marketing folks trying to be creative in the way they change the paradigm and add value to customer relations and increase total quality through a partnership with their clients. For example:

full service	total quality	family values
proactive	re-engineering	luxury
professional	consultant	all natural
creative	relationship	on sale
paradigm	rightsizing	sales training
value added	win-win	high-tech
customer relations	recycleable	partnership

There are a whole long list of others you can build once you understand the problem from the Buyer's point of view.

Because of their indefinite or complicated meanings, these words often leave larger implications of what isn't, rather than what is.

For instance, the word "creative" can raise serious doubts in a Buyer. As we used to say in the design business, "People who use the word 'creative,' ain't." Those who easily use the word (usually about themselves) are often the least creative. People who create for a living struggle with the word because it implies giving a star performance on demand under impossible conditions. Genuinely creative people know how hard it is to make rain by request.

You'll notice that professionals, consultants, politicians, motivational speakers, and advertising agencies love black-hole words; they think these words can't come back and bite them. Not true. Scary lawsuits with fangs spring from puffery.

Avoid black-hole words. From the Buyer's point of view they are heavy with baggage.

Representational statements:

"In the 15 years we have been in business, we have developed a response team that responds to our customers' calls within two hours."

"In a study of our industry, Metropolitan Business News *found that we were first in sales in our market."*

Puffery makes you look weak and not very bright. Representation makes you look strong and smart.

If you want to be believed, obey this law of the street:

LAW OF CREDIBILITY

**Don't say anything you can't prove.
Be able to prove everything you say.**

Every game needs some ground rules. Before building a presentation, we'll start out by telling the truth—Representation—and selling the right stuff—Benefits. We'll develop some elements that make you look honest and competent—Proof Statements. And we'll discuss how your business can be made unique and different from the competition.

9

FEATURES AND BENEFITS

Sell the right thing . . .

In any business, the only benefits that sell are **power, profit, prestige** and **pleasure,** or some permutation of these four basic human needs. Salespeople are mediocre at translating the Features of their product or service into Benefits for the Buyer—they end up trying to sell Features. By converting your business Features to Buyer Benefits, you can reposition your business to differentiate you from your competitors.

Features and Benefits are used throughout the selling presentation. In this Buyer-response form of selling, you'll use Benefits far more often than Features. The rules are:

- Features and Benefits always go together . . . like Mom and Dad or ham and eggs
- You may sell Benefits alone
- *Never* sell Features alone
- The more Benefits you sell, the more likely you are to close

---

Learn to sell Benefits to the Buyer, and you'll earn Benefits for yourself.

The Features are about your stuff, your products' or services' physical attributes—color, size, frequency, cost, activity, etc.

The Benefits are about the Buyers' stuff—what your products or services do for Buyers. Do the Benefits make them feel better about life—give them power; make them sexier, prettier, richer, more comfortable or secure, smarter, more competitive? Do they save time, money, fear or hassle?

Benefits move the dialog to the highest level of verbal communication—persuasion. Generally, Buyers are more interested in the Benefits of your product or service (in terms of power, profit, prestige, or pleasure) than in the Features of the product or service itself.

Any discussion of Features and Benefits can easily become an argument because they are really two different points of view. Simplify the discussion by asking the question, "Is what we are discussing for the Seller or the Buyer?" If for the Seller, it's a Feature; if for the Buyer, a Benefit.

Example of Features and Benefits

PanDowdy Computers:

Feature:

Model # 2100 SuperSpeed Computer Intuitive Interface

Benefits:

- Reduce training time per program by 30% (profit)
- Decrease downtime by 50% (profit, power)
- Reduce operator stress levels by half (profit, pleasure)

Feature:

Model #2100 compatible with both PanDowdy and IBM programs

Benefits:

- Choice of best programs yields increased productivity (power, profit)
- Maximum flexibility in business (power)
- Saves 25% of the investment in programs (profit)

You can tell the class of the salesperson by the Buyer Benefits used in the presentation.

Rocksolid Malpractice Insurance:

Feature:

24-hour approval for new-hire physicians

Benefit:

- Puts your new doctors in the treatment room six weeks sooner, creating up to $45,000 in practice revenue per new physician (profit)

Feature:

Aggressive claim management policy

Benefit:

- Settles 95% of all claims without an indemnity payment (profit, power, prestige)

- Eliminates four to five claims per year and subsequent complaints to the National Physicians Data Bank which can cost a doctor as much as $350,000 over five years (profit, prestige, pleasure)

Great Benefits = Great Salesperson.

Zoom Ball Bearing Company:

Feature:

Zoom TefSlick hardened surgical steel balls

Benefit:

- Lasts 10% longer and reduces bearing failure by 65% (profit, pleasure)

Feature:

Just-in-Time Inventory program

Benefit:

- Reduces paperwork, shipping, and warehousing costs by 10% or more (profit, pleasure)

Pinstripe Management Consulting:

Feature:

76 Years in Business

Benefit:

- Experience shortens the time needed to complete mergers and acquisitions by 43% (profit, pleasure, power, prestige)

Except for the Benefits you sell, nobody cares about your message.

Feature:

International operation

Benefit:

- Provides the same array of services to global companies and makes it easier for your offices to communicate with each other, saving time (profit, power, prestige)
- Helps avoid expensive delays and missteps that can add one to three years to the acquisition process (profit, pleasure)

To be heard and remembered by the Buyer, often Benefits must be quantified, that is, expressed in numbers, ratios, percentages, and dollars and cents.

Examples from other businesses:

Feature:

Home near public school

Benefits:

- Property maintains value
- Value increases 3% per year (profit, prestige)
- Convenience (pleasure)
- Safety for children (pleasure)
- Family neighborhood (profit, pleasure)

Feature:

The Uptown Fitness Club

Benefits:

- Save time: only 10 minutes away (profit, pleasure)
- Many exercise options (pleasure)
- Pleasant surroundings (pleasure)
- Member-oriented facility (pleasure, power)
- Prestige of upscale club (pleasure, power)
- Quality membership (pleasure, power, profit)
- Business opportunities with other members (profit, pleasure)
- Wide choice of equipment and courts (pleasure, prestige)

Feature:

"Cash Track Program": a business-loan plan for small businesses

Benefits:

- Increases efficiency by 6% (profit, pleasure)
- Speeds cash flow by 15% (profit)
- Offers quick answers that ease management worries (pleasure, power)
- Enhances competitiveness (power, pleasure)

We see many businesses caught up in the breathless race to create new features for their products and services. This continuous upgrade path winds through our economy because your Buyer demands it. Surprisingly, there is little long term selling advantage created by new features because they are usually matched by competitors within six months; sometimes within days.

Hot new features by themselves offer unreliable short-term advantage; perhaps even a disadvantage if not sold well. Selling your new unique Features can cost you money over the long run. However, these same new Features, combined with refined and persuasive Benefits, can create a reliable competitive edge. The Buyer is not persuaded until you translate your hot new Features into hot new Benefits.

When you become expert at this you may choose to use *only* Benefits quantified in dollars, percentages, or ratios. It's faster and easier for everyone; Buyers love to see and hear quantified Benefits because your presentation sounds so intelligent.

10.

THE PROOF STATEMENT

Looking good, sounding honest . . .

Use a Proof Statement whenever the Buyer expresses *doubt* about your product or service.

A Proof Statement is a statement containing facts, figures, testimonials, parallel circumstances, and anything else that is tangible, quantifiable, or real. It is good to use expert opinions from someone who does not have a direct involvement in your transaction. A Proof Statement is a material representation and the opposite of puffery.

When the Buyer expresses doubt about your presentation, program, benefits, company or math, you are compelled to use facts. The Buyer is directing you to deliver a Proof Statement. It can be used as part of your answer to a Buyer's objection to prove the Benefit you are selling.

The Proof Statement is constructed in the following fashion. First, *state* the Benefit (not the Feature) you are about to prove. Then *prove* that Benefit using facts, figures, opinion of experts in the field, testimonials of others in the industry, or other tangible information that

---

Say only what you can prove. Be ready to prove everything you say.

is quantifiable and real. Using those facts, *apply* the Benefit to the Buyer (personally, if possible).

Proof Statement components:

- *State* the Benefit you are going to prove.
- *Prove* the Benefit for the Buyer.
- *Apply* the Benefit to the Buyer.

A Proof Statement example:

"PanDowdy Computer can save you 65% of your computer support costs (State the Benefit) *according to an Iris & Company survey of 62 user firms* (Prove the Benefit). *In your firm, that can mean a time savings of 1,160 man-hours every year or about $45,000."* (Apply the Benefit to the Buyer.)

Using the Proof Statement helps you persuade in several ways. It makes you look honest. It also makes you look prepared and competent. Honesty, preparation, and competence—these traits take salespeople to the top. There is no way to stop them. On this level of sales, there is little competition.

The Proof Statement is such an obvious selling move one would think that most folks have their Proof Statements together. And of course they don't. Their Proof Statements are in the file cabinet back at the office

---

Proof Statements make you sound honest and competent as few other things can.

hiding under last week's moldy lunch bag in a ragged envelope labeled "Industry Stuff."

Salespeople sound remarkably incompetent when they sell in the accepted "shuck-and-jive" style. The verbal dancing—all those wonderful little tricks of syntax that sales managers devise—can be easily dropped with the development of some reasonable and logical Proof Statements. Puffery, that sudden burst of warm wind blowing unprovable claims, is the standard currency of ordinary salespeople. Puffery is the stuff sold to a suspicious public.

You've seen puffery in action. You are the Buyer. Flashing a big smile, the Seller says to you,

"You're making a terrific buy here and I think you are going to make a ton of money with this service. That's the reason we are Number One in the business."

You look back at all those shiny teeth and shake your head slowly, hoping your real feelings don't show. You don't believe anything. You understand it's only a salesperson trying to make a buck.

Same scene but this time the Seller says,

"This service has proven to work 84% of the time. A study published by the National Professional Services *magazine indicate that most services have only a 61% efficiency. That 23% difference will allow you to look at more year-end profits."*

As a Buyer, the Proof Statement responds directly to your doubt; it relates directly to your condition and shows how the product or service can solve your problem or answer a need.

Well-constructed Proof Statements dispense with puffery; they make the Seller credible. A study conducted in the Northeast found 75% of first-time Buyers bought because they believed the Seller was honest. Proof Statements make you look honest. But, if you want to be a crook, well-prepared Proof Statements can help you there, too.

Major companies with high-profile names still sell with shuck-and-jive. Imagine what they could achieve if they were prepared to prove everything they said. Unfortunately, today's Buyers expect you to puff them. They are rarely disappointed. There is no faster way to break trust with the Buyer than to say that you or your company is "Number One" or "the best." This is such a phony ploy that inside, your Buyer is laughing at you. Occasionally the Buyer is even less subtle. Sometimes they will laugh right in your face.

Don't puff. Relying on puffery is a dangerous and expensive game. Misrepresentation (that can develop into lawsuit) is easy when you are puffing. Develop a Proof Statement that goes with the answer to each Buyer's objection. You should also have one for every representation you make about the Benefits of your product or service.

Proof Statement examples:

The Buyer says:

"I'm not sure your product is as good as you say."

You say:

"The Acme Autoslotter can save you time and money (The Benefit you are going to prove). World Hardware Magazine *said the Acme is 22% more efficient to operate* (Proved the benefit quoting an accepted source). *That saves you time that you can use to increase profits in other areas."* (Applied the Benefit to the Buyer.**)**

Rocksolid Malpractice Insurance:

The Buyer says:

"How do we profit from your insurance coverage?"

You say:

"Rocksolid's services increase profits for medical groups and hospitals (Benefit you are going to prove). *Mercy Hospital in Berry, Rhode Island saved $27,000 in direct costs of risk management while increasing managed care services by 8%* (Proved the Benefit quoting an accepted source). *This range of services can increase profits 20% to 30% for medical groups like yours while helping you practice better medicine."* (Applied the Benefit to the Buyer.)

Zoom Roller Bearing:

"Zoom TefSlick bearings can reduce your assembly line downtime. (Benefit you are going to prove) Metallurgical Testing Magazine *showed that surgical steel balls gave 10% longer wear than competitive brands.* (Proved the Benefit quoting an accepted source.) *That 10% longer wear means about a 2% gain in total assembly line production for your company."* (Applied Benefit to the Buyer.)

Often, the Buyer is shopping for a salesperson, not a specific company or a product.

Pinstripe Management Consulting:

"Pinstripe can help you shorten your merger time (Benefit you are going to prove). *With our last three Fortune 500 clients, we were able to shorten their merger time by an average of 43%* (Proved the Benefit). *That means you can get your company productive after merger and save nearly four months of downtime that usually occurs while people figure out their new job."* (Applied the Benefit to the Buyer.)

A final note: It might seem there are few Proof Statements you can use when selling ideas.

"But *ideas* don't have solid proofs available," you say.

Of course they do. They have renderings, projections, market studies, other related ideas, case histories, pro formas, and opinions from disinterested experts. Selling ideas is the most fun. If properly prepared and presented, an idea is the most exciting product in our culture. Ideas fire the imagination and allow Buyers to become involved with their own concept of how the idea might apply. Just because an idea doesn't exist on the physical plane doesn't mean it need be vaguely presented.

Three Underlying Assumptions

To build a powerful, honest presentation suitable to any profession, whether you are a bricklayer or an actuary, design your presentation around the following underlying assumptions.

Use:

- "You" not "I"

  (Focus on your Buyer.)

- Representation, with proof, not Puffery

  (Don't tell lies.)

- Benefits not Features

  (Sell the right thing.)

11.

MARKET DIFFERENTIATION

Sounding like the Joneses . . .

Market differentiation allows you to position your selling effort so that your product, service, or company shows up as a separate entity from all your competitors.

Let's complete another short exercise. In 40 words or less, and without puffing, write a statement explaining how your product, service, or company is provably different from your competitors:

In your Marketing Statement . . .

- Did you use puff words like "the best . . .," "Number One . . .," "only . . .," "honest . . .," etc., that aren't provable?

- Did you quantify and prove everything in your statement?

- Does it contain a compelling Benefit for the Buyer?

If your business is similar to your competitor's, don't be discouraged. Ultimately, the Buyer's perception of differences between one business and another hinges on how well they are treated by the salespeople. Buyers shop for salespeople more than anything else.

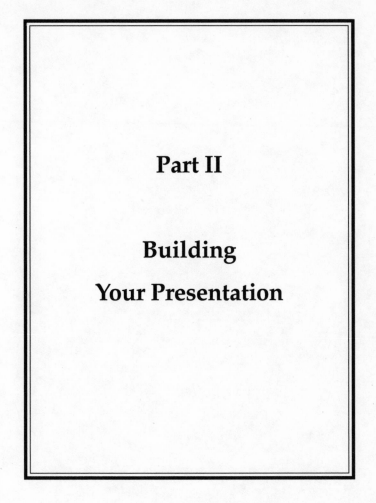

Part II

Building
Your Presentation

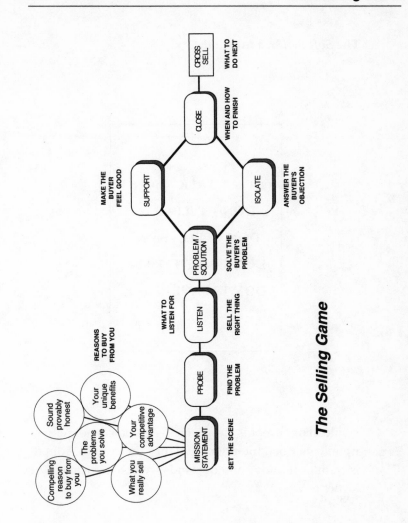

The Selling Game

The *Soft Sell* in a nutshell:

DON'T TALK - Listen

DON'T TELL - Ask

DON'T SELL - Solve

DON'T PITCH - Probe

DON'T LEAVE - Close

While this concept is simple enough, you cannot rely upon your good intentions and intuition to pull it off; it is counter-intuitive and demands well-constructed tactics to work.

12

THE SEVEN SELLING MOVES

The basic structure of the Soft Sell . . .

Just as a carpenter has tools to work his chosen profession, a salesperson has tools to work the trade of persuasion. Salespeople confuse their great ambition, perfect attitude and working knowledge of a product or service with the basic tools of the profession. It's like the carpenter mistaking the desire to build a house for the implements required for its construction. Once these tools are mastered the carpenter may build an outhouse or a castle, depending on skill, talent, vision, attention, and luck.

The Seller has similar tools that encourage the Buyer to author the sale, to feel important and yes, even to like the Seller while doing so. These seven moves—Mission Statement, Probe, Listen, Problem/Solution, Isolate, Support, Close—are hammer and saw for the persuader. Now that you've learned the difference between Puffery and Representation, Features and Benefits, and Proof Statements to differentiate your product or service from your competitors, you can use these tools to position your *Soft Selling* presentation.

The first duty of the salesperson is to survive the presentation, that is, keep the meeting alive long enough to find a Buyer's problem to solve. The second duty is to solve the problem and close the sale as painlessly as possible for both Buyer and Seller. To perform these two difficult duties, the Seller's moves need to be designed in advance. This section shows why and how to prepare the basic technical moves required in the *Soft Sell*.

We will use examples of fictional companies throughout to give you a sense of how the moves are built for different products and services. Our examples are for ball bearings (usually considered to be a commodity), medical liability insurance, personal computers, and professional consulting services. We've also included some random examples. Note that the illustrations are generic and simplified to reveal the structure of each move so you may apply the mechanics to your own stuff.

Selling Move #1

Mission Statement

The Mission Statement introduces you to the Buyer.

As modern business moves faster, there is less time to schmooze the Buyers. They are rushed. Their attention is short. Until you have established trust and a working relationship, the personal side of the sales call suffers. A sale can happen in 90 seconds. Sometimes it takes years to make a trusting friend.

A Mission Statement is a snapshot of your business; it sets the scene for a cold call, a first meeting, or the meeting agenda. It's your story in 40 words or less that explains why you are taking up the Buyer's valuable time. It often explains your real business—the *Benefits* you sell in the marketplace. It's also used to introduce yourself on a cold call, any time you are asked about your business, or as an opening line in requesting an appointment by telephone.

The Mission Statement covers the following:
- Your name and/or company name
- Your business objectives, i.e. why you are taking up the Buyer's time
- What kinds of problems you solve
- The benefits of your solution

It is easier to make a sale than a friend.

A Mission Statement example:

"My name is Nigel Furn from HighNoon Refoliators. We help home owners reduce water usage for lawn care and save them up to 50% in irrigation costs."

A Mission Statement isn't particularly easy to write. Sometimes it takes a year or more. Most of us are so involved with our product or service we don't stop to decide exactly what we do from the Buyer's point-of-view. There's the rub. Our interest lies in our own products and services. Conversely, Buyers are only interested in what's in it for them.

As the tempo of business quickens each year, you have a painfully short time to make the kazanga-leap from being "just another salesperson" to being a trusted problem-solver for the Buyer. About four minutes. Every word you say must pay off in trust and professionalism. You buy your way in with Benefits to capture the Buyer's attention. Opening with a Mission Statement sets the scene for the conversation to come. As long as you are talking about Benefits for the Buyer (you'll notice I didn't use the "F" word—"Features"), you have the Buyer's full attention from the first word. When you come through the door offering Benefits rather than some lame attempt to make small talk on the Buyer's busy time, you look and sound more professional. While we salespeople are wonderful, warm, sensitive, and caring human beings, these days we only get to show that by talking about the Buyer's Benefits. You can always make friends and talk about the Buyer's kids, kitty, and sailboat later. After the sale is made.

Of the Mission Statement elements, your name and company are the least important. For the purposes of brevity you can leave them out if you like. Your Buyer doesn't care who you are or where you're from until you have established that you carry important problem-solving solutions. The Buyer will then ask your name and hear it, even scribble it down on a scrap of paper. Yeah!

Some Mission Statement examples:

"PanDowdy builds computers designed to help you increase your company's productive computer time by as much as 23%."

"Rocksolid Malpractice Insurance provides protection for medical groups that can increase annual revenues $12,000 to $20,000 per physician."

*"Zoom Ball Bearing makes TefSlick bearings that help
manufacturers keep their assembly lines moving as much as
200 addtional hours a year."*

*"Pinstripe Management Consulting helps growing compa-
nies reduce by 43% the time required to make new corporate acquisitions profitable."*

You will notice that the common elements of Mission
Statements are that they are short, to the point, use or
allude to numbers, and create a clear snapshot of your
business.

To help your Buyer understand what you do, obey this
street law:

LAW OF CLARITY

**If you can't explain what you sell to a ten-year-old
child then you don't know what you sell.**

Selling Move #2

Probes

Our culture is an impolite one and questions normally
asked the Buyer are frontal, i.e., tactless, adversarial and
accusative. Common questions usually start with some
form of the verb "to be":

*"Will you . . . Have you . . . Can you . . . Won't you . . .
Are you . . . Is this . . . Were they . . . Should you . . .
Would you . . . Could you . . . etc. "*

The Seller usually charges directly at the point with the subtlety of a troop of Boy Scouts. While these questions sound culturally acceptable, they aren't persuasion. Until trained to question well, ordinary salespeople attack the Buyer with Frontal probes. (Yes, dear reader, I am talking about you.)

Sometimes they attempt to set clumsy traps using contractions to lead the Buyer into a favorable answer: *"Wouldn't you like to be the first person in your industry to use this ground-breaking technology?"*

There is plenty of room for subtlety in selling. A key component of the *Soft Sell* is asking questions that require the Buyer to think and reach inside for the answer so as to reveal needs the Seller can fulfill with a product or service.

There are two types of probes:

- **Frontal probes** fly directly into the Buyer's armor— *"Mr. Rogers, are you the decision-maker for the company?"*

- **Flanking probes** get behind the Buyer's armor— *"Mr. Rogers, how are decisions like this made inside your firm?"*

When we play our Buyer's role, each of us is armor-plated.

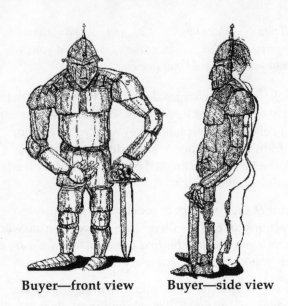

Buyer—front view   **Buyer—side view**

Frontal probes are questions that can be answered with a single word. These probes are generally used when the Seller attacks the Buyer. (Not on purpose, of course. Ordinary salespeople protest with inarguable certainty that they are "only requesting specific information!") The problem arises because the Buyer's defensive agents are perfectly prepared to resist the Seller—to give a negative answer if possible. Frontal probes are tactless. They sound like attacks, or at least challenges. It's difficult not to sound adversarial using Frontal probes. It's how the Buyer's armor got built.

Ordinary salespeople are poor information gatherers. They believe they ask questions that gain information about the Buyer except that they nearly always use Frontal probes that force the Buyer into areas of the Seller's interest. Forcing the Buyer into those restricted areas seriously limits the Seller's opportunity to uncover Buyer information upon which an agreement can be struck. Frontal probes restrict both the area of conversation and the range of the Buyer's imagination. Since the questions usually call for a one-word answer (usually yes or no), the Seller must be very precise about the information that is needed. The Seller must carry the conversational burden since a one-word answer relieves the Buyer of having to think much. Frontal probes make the Seller work like crazy. And the more the Seller works, the harder it is to close softly.

The Buyer is used to yes-or-no questions not only from salespeople but from everyone. With Frontal probes, the Buyer has a ready answer even before the question is fully asked. The answer comes from outside the Buyer. It's quick and automatic and unhelpful in building a sales presentation because every salesperson asks it.

Flanking probes are used whenever the Seller wants to discover what the Buyer needs or wants; uncover the Buyer's dissatisfaction with current products or services; allow the Buyer to express opinions about anything; and encourage the Buyer to discuss problems or needs without threat. In the *Soft Sell*, Flanking probes allow the Buyer and Seller to be non-adversarial.

Flanking probes work because the Buyer isn't used to being asked non-manipulative questions. The Buyer relaxes because the probe doesn't contain implications that the Buyer made poor decisions in the past or will in the future. The Buyer becomes non-defensive in giving information especially when you make the Buyer feel good, that is, support at every opportunity. By answering openly, the Buyer carries the burden of the presentation. The Seller has plenty of time to listen and think.

A Flanking probe requires the Buyer to search for the answer, make decisions, and create an opinion. It takes the Buyer off "automatic" and onto "think." The Buyer must go inside to develop a reasonable and well-thought answer. Usually that mind search takes some time. So, if the Buyer answers quickly, the probe is probably a Frontal probe.

Obviously, getting behind the Buyer's armor with Flanking probes is more effective. It makes the Seller

---

When selling, the obvious is rarely enough. Look beyond the obvious to get to the Buyer's need.

look smart, gets the Buyer to speak easily, and gives the Seller the information needed without threatening the Buyer. It is the non-adversarial way of asking questions.

Another expensive habit of ordinary salespeople is to ask several questions in a row, without letting the Buyer answer, and then guess at the answer (or add other questions as an afterthought) which limits the Buyer's response. This is called a "Run-on question."

A "Run-on question" example:

"Ms. Wilson, has that category been selling well for you? . . . have you been happy with it? . . . or not? . . . is it the right model for your customers? . . . or do they ask for something else? . . . another brand perhaps?"

If salespeople don't probe well for background information, they don't know how to launch the presentation. When salespeople don't know what to do, they talk. The ordinary salesperson vomits the presentation onto the Buyer's desk top. Only rarely will a salesperson ask a question that allows the Buyer to get involved, make decisions, or help author the sale.

Proper preparation of carefully constructed probes converts a mundane, lusterless presentation into one where Buyers carry the burden and feel good about themselves, the Seller and the decision that has been made, and give the Seller more information than is needed to close.

Flanking probes start with one of these words: *who, how, what, why, when, where*. For instance, you sell software and you ask:

> *"Ms. Quigley, how's the new computer system impacting your business?"*

Ms. Quigley now has the opportunity to vent her spleen about the new system. Because Flanking probes are not specific, she will talk about the parts of the system that are important to her—what it does right and what it does wrong. Like most of us, she is rarely asked her opinion by anyone, so her answers will be honest. Now, sit back and listen for opportunities to give Supporting Statements. Ms. Quigley feels good about giving her opinions and you continue to make her feel good as you introduce Benefits of your product or service.

Flanking probes encourage self-expression on the Buyer's part. They keep the Seller from playing fortune teller: "Let me gaze deeply into my crystal ball and tell you what your future holds. Ahhhh, it holds exactly what I am selling. Isn't that amazing?"

Ordinary salespeople endlessly play a game called "Let Me Guess." Instead of probing to determine the Buyer's attitudes and opinions, problems and needs, the Seller guesses at them and designs solutions using guesswork as gospel. (A method called "Ready, Fire! Aim.") More often than not, the Seller guesses wrong—trying to fill a need that doesn't exist, or hasn't been created, in the Buyer's mind. Don't guess at the Buyer's need—ask Flanking probes.

Buyer's defensive agents aren't equipped to defend against intelligent questions requesting an opinion. For most of their lives, Buyers have been asked stupid questions requiring simple yes-or-no answers. They are experts in giving stupid Sellers "no" answers. Sellers must ask questions that make the Buyer go inside for the answer.

You, the Seller, are looking for silence from the Buyer, some quiet time in which they generate well considered answers. Fast answers from the Buyer work against your interest and are a symptom that you asked a Frontal question.

Four Probes to Prepare

While developing Flanking probes isn't rocket science, they do need to be prepared word for word. There are four types of probes for the Seller to prepare.

- **Standard Probes:**
  Questions asked initially of all new Buyers.

- **Best of All Possible Worlds Probes:**
  Questions that allow the Buyer to dream.

- **Emergency Probes:**
  Questions asked when the Seller is pressed, stressed, lost or confused.

- **Status Quo Probes:**
  Questions that uncover areas of dissatisfaction with what the Buyer is doing now.

Standard Probes

Standard probes are questions asked during each meeting with a new Buyer. They can be used to establish rapport, gain basic information, qualify the Buyer and set up Supporting Statements that make the Buyer feel important.

Use Standard probes during the first few minutes of a sales appointment. Then sprinkle them throughout the meeting whenever they are needed to gain valuable information.

A Standard probe that flanks the Buyer's armor is difficult for the Buyer to defend against. The Buyer isn't used to hearing intelligent questions, thus has few defensive agents trained to protect against them.

The **Standard probe (Flanking)** begins with *who, how, what, when, why,* or *where* and asks the Buyer to stop, think, quantify, and make decisions. The probe is tactful, non-adversarial, and does not imply that the Buyer has made poor decisions in the past, is currently wrong, or has a disastrous future if the Buyer continues on the present course.

Standard Flanking probe examples (with Frontal examples in parentheses):

PanDowdy Computer:

"How are you using personal computers to enhance your business?" (*"Do you use personal computers in your company?"*)

Rocksolid Malpractice Insurance:

"How is managed care impacting practice revenues?" ("Are you paying too much in premiums?")

Zoom Ball Bearing:

"How has your company maintained its market share with all the turmoil in Asia?" ("Are you losing business in Asia?")

Pinstripe Management Consulting:

"In your department, what is the toughest part in acquiring a new company?" ("Is buying a new company difficult for you?")

Standard Flanking probe examples from other businesses:

"How does your business compare with your projections from a year ago?" ("Is business good?")

"What factors do you feel help your company remain successful?" ("Are you staying competitive?")

"Who will be the person in charge of this program?" ("Are you in charge here?")

"Ideally, what would you like the real estate to do for you?" ("What type of house are you looking for?")

"What categories are best sellers in that department?" ("Are you doing well in that category?")

"When do you feel would be the best time to get started?" ("Do you want to start now?")

"What kind of marketing program do you prefer?" ("Is your advertising working?")

"How are buying decisions made inside your firm?" ("Are you the decision-maker in the company?")

Flanking probes turn an ordinary sales call into an easy exchange of information, builds trust, and quickly bonds the Seller to the Buyer.

Best of All Possible Worlds Probe

The Best of All Possible Worlds question allows the Buyer to dream, that is, it gives the Buyer the opportunity to design or imagine the perfect transaction.

Sellers use this probe whenever they need the Buyer to imagine the ideal situation; to bring the transaction to a quick and satisfactory conclusion; to build a checklist of the Buyer's requirements; or to build trust with the Buyer.

Ordinary salespeople are afraid to use the Best of All Possible Worlds probe because they are sure the Buyer will ask for things the Seller is unable to deliver. In our

Ask a Best of All Possible Worlds probe well and the result is a flattered Buyer.

culture, ordinary salespeople don't allow Buyers to wander off into their own areas of interest. Salespeople vomit their presentation rather than allow Buyers to become involved. While the Best of All Possible Worlds probe looks obvious, it is rarely used. Often, it is the first time a Buyer's opinion has ever been asked for.

Best of All Possible World examples for:

PanDowdy Computer:

"What would you like the perfect computer system to do for your company?"

Rocksolid Malpractice Insurance Company:

"If it was within your power, how would you go about protecting your physicians against lawsuits?"

Zoom Ball Bearing Company:

"Assuming you could do anything you wanted, what would be your best-of-all-possible-worlds scenario for this transaction?"

Pinstripe Management Consulting:

"From your point of view, what would the perfect business acquisition look like?"

Other businesses:

"Ms. Buyer, if you could design this transaction any way you would like it, how would it look?"

"In the best of all possible worlds, if you could build the perfect situation without constraints of time or money, what would it look like?"

The Best of All Possible Worlds probe is most likely the best probe with which to make things happen. It is a deal-making probe.

Emergency Probes

When in trouble, the natural response for salespeople is to talk. The Emergency probe reverses the compulsion to babble to an unwilling Buyer. It poses an intelligent question that disturbs the pace of the Buyer's attack or adversarial train of thought.

The Emergency probe is used whenever the Seller is pressed, stressed, lost or confused, such as when you . . .

- Lose your place in the presentation

- Can't remember what to do next

- Are under attack by the Buyer

- Find the presentation is moving too fast and you need time to gather your thoughts

---

If you ask questions the same old way, the Buyers become defensive in spite of themselves.

It is a question that . . .

- Flanks the Buyer's armor
- Is complex
- Calls for a well-considered answer
- Begins with who, how, what, when, or where
- Places the burden of the interview back on the Buyer
- Makes the Buyer stop, think and quantify an answer
- Is designed to buy you time

Emergency probe examples:

"Ms. Jones, exactly what will it take to make you happy in this case?"

"In the best of all possible worlds, if you could structure this transaction any way you would like, how would you design it?"

"Allow me to ask you, exactly where did I go wrong?"

"I seem to have gotten off track. Help me get back to what is most important to you."

Some humility can go a long way to ease the tension when the Seller is in difficulty with a Buyer.

Status Quo Probes

Status Quo probes are used whenever Buyers are happy with what they are doing now (which is much of the time). These probes are designed to uncover the Buyer's dissatisfaction with a current product or service. Once you have discovered those hidden dissatisfactions or needs, then, obviously, sell into those needs.

The Seller uses Status Quo probes whenever the Buyer responds in the following way:

"I'm happy with what I am doing now."

"I have no need for your product or service."

"I don't have the time to talk to you."

"Call me later."

"Don't call me ever again."

The Status Quo probe works because when facing rejection, most salespeople aren't prepared to ask the Buyer questions but to simply accept, at face value, whatever the Buyer says. The cultural response is to spew out the sales presentation in the hopes that the Buyer will discover something of interest.

For instance, commercial real estate brokers often hear *"I already have a broker"* from their prospects, yet studies show that this is a stalling tactic 75%-90% of the time—

what the prospect says isn't true. It is customary in that business to turn and walk as soon as you hear this from a prospect rather than ask some Status Quo probes to develop some interest.

The Buyer has few defenses against intelligent and tactful Status Quo probes.

The Status Quo probe is used . . .

- To uncover needs that may be unknown to the Buyer
- To gain the Buyer's attention when time is precious
- To detect weaknesses in the competitor's products or services
- To set up a Closing Statement

Status Quo probe examples:

PanDowdy Computer:

"How does computer downtime impact your peoples' stress levels?"

"How do you use personal computers to sharpen your competitive edge?"

Rocksolid Malpractice Insurance:

"How are you managing liability risk to increase patient satisfaction and practice revenues?"

Zoom Ball Bearing:

"How are you taking advantage of foreign market turmoil to increase revenues?"

"What strategy have you implemented to prevent erosion of your market share?"

Pinstripe Management Consulting:

"How are you minimizing key employee turnover during this merger?"

Other Businesses:

"How has your job been affected by your physical condition?"

"How long since you've had the natural high from exercising?"

"What arrangements do you make to show your property while you are away?"

"How has your life-style been affected by changes in the neighborhood?"

"How do you keep your competition from setting your price?"

"Generally speaking, how close have you come to the profit goals you set for your firm?"

"How do you ensure a zero defect rate in your sales presentations?"

When making cold calls, Status Quo probes are the Seller's source of new Buyers and new income.

Which Probe to Use When?

As a probing plan, probe for what the Buyer is doing now (Standard and Status Quo) then probe on what the Buyer would like to be doing in the future (Best of All Possible Worlds). Finally, determine the barrier that keeps the Buyer from achieving their best of all possible worlds. The barrier that keeps the Buyer from reaching his or her goal is the focal point of the sale.

A Frontal probe is the tool of last resort when Flanking probes are failing to give you open responses. If Flanking probes are not working, use Frontal probes. As a probing tactic, if you do not get usable responses after two or three Flanking probes, change to Frontal probes; then shift back to Flanking probes as soon as the Buyer's responses and attitude allow it.

A sale often turns on a single, well-developed Flanking probe. The Seller who asks thought-provoking, intelligent questions and then listens to the answers has the power, the time, and the control in the interview.

Selling Move #3

Listening

Fifty percent of successful selling is Listening. After asking a carefully crafted question, you must listen skillfully to the answer and decide whether the answer helps your cause or hinders it.

- If the answer "helps your cause," you **Support** and **Close** (We're coming to these moves soon.)

- If the answer goes "against your cause," you **Isolate** the Buyer's objection, answer it, and when you get agreement, **Close**

Listening with Three Ears

Listening is a whole body effort. Great salespeople expend more energy paying attention to what the Buyer says than to any other effort.

To excel as a professional salesperson, when the Buyer speaks you must (Yes, "must") listen to . . .

- What **is** being said—without introducing your personal desires

- What **is not** being said—because everything the Buyer says implies another side

- What **cannot** be said—because of internal politics, inability to articulate, etc.

Expert Listening Skills

Listening skills underlie selling skills. The best sales-people are the best listeners and do four things consistently.

1. **Devote full attention** to the speaker, are not preoccupied, control their emotions, don't interrupt, and don't fill in blanks for the speaker.

2. Use the **speed of thought** (which is five times faster than speaking) to enter their own experience to validate what speaker is saying.

3. **Determine the organization** in the speaker's mind.

4. **Create solutions, not rebuttals.**

When you create solutions for the Buyer you are working for the Buyer's interest. The word "but" signals the Buyer that you are about to argue. Don't use the word "but."

Levels of Verbal Communication

It seems most misunderstandings occur because people work on different levels of communication within the same transaction. There are four levels of verbal communication. Be sure you are on the same level as the

If you are not listening, you are losing.

Buyer. If you are not, persuasion is difficult or impossible.

Level 1. **Small talk**—the amenities, chitchat, the **bonding** between humans occurs at this level.

Level 2. **Catharsis**—the **sharing of feeling** and opinion, emotional insight.

Level 3. **Exchange of information**—the transfer of knowledge. In sales: **exploring the Features.**

Level 4. **Persuasion**—making or changing opinion. In sales: **discussing the Benefits.**

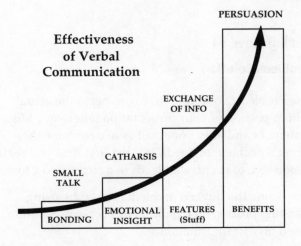

If you are not on the same level of communication with your Buyer, you will pass like ships in the night.

It's easy to see why Feature-only presentations are ineffective. Features keep the Buyer at a lower level of verbal communication. Benefits work because they take the Buyer to the highest level of communication—persuasion.

The difficulty of "selling yourself first" is exposed here—it keeps you at the small talk level when you want to be at the persuasion level. Yes, bonding occurs at the first level but persuasion happens three levels above. If selling for you is a rocky road, convert your presentation to a series of Benefits. It'll go easier for you and your Buyer will love it. After all, at the persuasion level the meeting is totally about the Buyer. Very unusual.

Selling Move #4

Problem/Solution

The Problem/Solution is a way to begin the actual selling portion of your presentation (after your Mission Statement and after your probes to determine the Buyer's problem or need). It is the first time you set up a sequence of events that leads to a structured Close.

Determine the Buyer's problem or need by using Flanking probes, then build your Problem/Solution based on that information.

Construct the Problem/Solution statement so it moves from a general condition to the specific application of your product or service.

In designing this move . . .

- Your statement moves from the Buyer's need or *problem* to your *solution*

- Your product or service *name* is offered as the solution or answer to the Buyer's problem or need

- The *Benefit* of your solution is included

Don't confuse the Problem/Solution with the Mission Statement.

The Mission Statement introduces you to the Buyer and furnishes context for the meeting. The Problem/Solution responds to the Buyer's particular problem or need and prepares the conditions for the Buyer's commitment.

A Problem/Solution example:

"Mr. Tarmac, highway supervisors are spending more of their budget keeping our roadsides clean (Buyer's problem). *The Acme Road Vacuum sucks up roadside trash and automatically sorts it saving you 22% in employee wages and management expense."* (Your solution and Benefit.)

The Problem/Solution moves from the Buyer's problem to your product or service as a solution, and that solution includes a Benefit for the Buyer. Designed correctly, the next probe naturally sets up a Closing Probe.

Problem/Solution examples:

PanDowdy Computer:

"Paying technical people to keep your personal computers on-line can multiply the total cost of operations by three times (Buyer's problem). *PanDowdy can reduce support by as much as 65% and save you $45,000 in employee costs allowing you to redirect a large part of your support budget to more productive uses."* (Your solution and Benefit.)

Rocksolid Malpractice Insurance:

"Managed care forces your doctors to see 25% more patients to maintain their practice revenues. This high patient load increases the risk of malpractice claims (Buyer's problem). *Rocksolid's risk management plan increases staff efficiency and patient satisfaction while reducing the risk of missed diagnosis or documentation errors saving up to $30,000 per year in direct costs."* (Your solution and Benefit.)

Zoom Ball Bearing:

*"Bearing failures can cost a manufacturer as much 205
hours a year in assembly line downtime* (Buyer's problem). *Zoom's TefSlick Bearings are especially hardened to
reduce bearing failure by 65% keeping assembly lines
running longer and more trouble free."* (Your solution
and Benefit.)

Pinstripe Management Consulting:

*"Poor communications with employees can drain your time
and personnel resources and make your department look
incompetent* (Buyer's problem). *Our process improve-
ment techniques streamline communications and free up
your people to do their main job by eliminating 90% of
your employee's questions and misunderstandings."* (Your
solution and Benefit.)

Other businesses:

*"With a single personal banker, your business options can
depend on that person's limited experience* (Buyer's
problem). *Our widely experienced team of specialists at
Intergalactic National Bank gives you many management
options when making important business decisions."* (Your
solution and Benefit.)

"Studies show that the closer your home is located to the club, the more you'll use it (Buyer's problem). *The Uptown Fitness Club is only four blocks from your apartment so you can work out every afternoon, look terrific and save 10 hours a month in travel time."* (Your solution and Benefit.)

"A constant parade of prospects prowling through your house is disruptive (Buyer's problem). *At Goin'deMax Realty, we pre-qualify every prospect so you don't get hassled to show your property to people who are just looking."* (Your solution and Benefit.)

"When you hire your competitors' salespeople, your selling presentations sound exactly like theirs (Buyer's problem). *In the VASS® EXECUTIVE SALES TRAINING course, we develop a presentation that separates your company's image from your competitors and increases your market recognition by 30%."* (Your solution and Benefit.)

The Problem/Solution is based directly on the Buyer's problem or need. With the correct Flanking probe tacked on, it can turn into a 90-Second Close, an advanced selling tactic explained later on.

Selling Move #5

Supporting Statements

When playing games, winning free shots or bonus points can make the difference between winning or losing. The Supporting Statement is your free shot in a presentation. Everything else in sales must be worked at or set up—earned. Since selling is a game and the Supporting Statement is a free shot, obviously, all salespeople take their freebies at every opportunity, right? Wrong. Few salespeople use this, the most effective and economical selling tool in their kit.

Use a Supporting Statement each time the Buyer says something that helps your cause. The Supporting Statement makes the Buyer feel good and, therefore, you too. Why? In selling you work with a basic emotion—the Buyer's need to feel correct. When the Buyer feels correct, you are rewarded.

The Buyer's hard sell defensive agents aren't alert to this kind of treatment from salespeople. Buyers are used to being attacked. Of the 61,000 daily advertising messages engulfing the Buyer, each implies the Buyer made a wrong decision (driving the wrong car, buying the wrong toothpaste, wearing the wrong clothes, etc.).

The Buyer is often wrong. You don't have to agree.

A Supporting Statement catches the Buyer doing something right and creates an exchange of self-esteem between you and the Buyer and opens the door to the Buyer's mind. It makes you friends, builds trust and differentiates you from your competitors. The Supporting Statement is the hinge on the door of the *Soft Sell*.

The Buyer's statement doesn't have to be stated positively; it can be a negative comment about your competitors or something negative about the Buyer's own situation that you can help.

In our culture, salespeople are trained to attack, either overtly or covertly, rather than support the customer. Supporting Statements get behind the Buyer's armor quickly and open the door to the Buyer's mind. This practice is so uncommon that when done well, the Buyer rarely perceives it. This selling move fulfills a basic human need: the need to be right.

Being told they are right is so out of character in our culture, Buyers can hardly wait to hear why they are correct. It opens the door to Buyers' minds. Their attention becomes riveted to your next statement as you are about to fulfill a basic need. Even if interrupted at this point, they will quickly bring you back to the subject at hand—their correctness. When the Buyers' attention is focused, a benefit of your product or service can be clearly received by Buyers without the interfer-

---

Our cultural agreement is "The Seller Attacks — The Buyer Defends."

ence of the mental background noise they usually carry with them. The Buyer hears you.

We are accustomed to being told we are right. Right? Here's a little test. How long has it been since you were looked directly in the eye by anyone and told you were right? Among my students, answers of a year or more are common. Supporting Statements are so rare that they are clearly remembered a year later. The pleasant memory is a testimony to their effectiveness. It's likely you can remember Supporting Statements from your childhood. Incidentally, people at the top of the selling trade use Supporting Statements more than usual; the best of them rarely lose an opportunity to make the Buyer feel important.

In reality, the Buyer is often wrong. Do not support statements made against your cause. Everyone has heard the old adage, "The customer is always right." Ordinary salespeople feel compelled to agree with the Buyer no matter how silly or misinformed the Buyer's argument is. If the Buyer is wrong, don't agree. Don't argue. Don't do anything except acknowledge the comment with something like "I understand." (Note: This is one of the few times the pronoun "I" is permissible when selling.) It sounds insensitive but in use, handled in a casual conversational style, the Buyer seldom notices your lack of agreement. You can disagree without being disagreeable or drawing attention to the disagreement. The real message from the disagreement is that it reveals the Buyer's objection. After answering the objection, you can close.

In forming a Supporting Statement, first, you agree with the Buyer's statement—something as simple as "You're right" works just fine. Second, you give a Benefit of your product or service.

1. Agree with the Buyer.

2. Give a Benefit of your product or service.

For example, the Buyer says:

"Our industry has had difficulty maintaining a steady growth over the past three years."

The Seller returns:

"Yes, you are right, (Agreed with Buyer). *The industry is suffering a downturn. Paying too much for insurance services hasn't helped either. That's why InterState Insurance has devised a program that will help you save 15% on your premiums."* (Gave an additional Benefit.)

Examples of Supporting Statements:

PanDowdy Computer:

"You are right, systems support is a major headache and a pure cost (Agreed). *PanDowdy minimizes the support time and people and allows your users to stay on-line 94% of the year."* (Additional Benefit.)

Rocksolid Malpractice Insurance:

"You are right, malpractice claims can be very expensive (Agreed). *Dr. Robert Boldway calculated that one claim reported to the National Physician's Data Bank cost him $77,000 per year for five years or $385,000 in lost revenue as well as thirty agonizing days out of the treatment room and in the court room."* (Additional Benefit.)

Zoom Ball Bearing Company:

"You're right. Overstocking can eat up warehouse space (Agreed). *Using just-in-time inventory methods can eliminate surplus inventory and save you 12%, or more, in warehousing costs."* (Additional Benefit.)

Pinstripe Management Consulting:

"You're right. Business mergers present unexpected problems on a daily basis (Agreed). *Our change management team has been through this process 23 times in the last five years and can help you anticipate and resolve key*

issues so your management stress is reduced and you sleep better at night." (Additional Benefit.)

Supporting Statements from other businesses:

"*Yes, you're right, Ms. Jones. This home does have a lovely kitchen* (Agreed). *And it's only two blocks from the elementary school giving you the sense of safety you wanted.*" (Additional Benefit.)

"*You're right, Marie. Disciplined people like you understand that regular exercise workouts improve your outlook* (Agreed). *They suppress your appetite, too, helps you lose six pounds a month and allows you to feel better about life.*" (Additional Benefit.)

And Supporting Statements are an excellent test of how well you are listening. You cannot support Buyers correctly if you are not carefully listening to what they say.

Support quickly and concisely. Don't linger or make a big deal about agreeing. A simple "You're right," is sufficient to open the door. It flanks the Buyer's defensive agents. In tests with Buyers, the Seller used "You're right," as many as forty-five times in one hour without getting caught. Did she close? What do you think?

Support people. Attack problems.

Here are some other ways you can agree with the Buyer:

- That's great . . .
- Fine . . .
- Right . . .
- You're correct . . .
- That's true . . .
- You're assumptions are correct . . .
- Your concerns are well-founded . . .
- Absolutely correct . . .
- Indeed . . .
- The experts agree with you . . .
- That's very astute . . .
- That has been our other clients' experience . . .

Support the Buyer's *human* accomplishments such as:

- Good business instincts
- Ambition
- Discipline
- Control of the situation
- Good management skills
- Vision
- Skill
- Knowledge

- Planning
- Luck
- Aggressiveness
- Creativity

You can support difficulties caused by your competition as long as your statement doesn't include personal or business criticism of the competitor. It works best if you don't mention the competitor at all but discuss only the problems created by competitors' products or services. (And don't talk about what a good guy the competitor is or how good his competition is. It makes you support going the wrong way. It can dig a deep hole from which it can be impossible to climb out.)

Some typical problems your competitor might have:

- Leaves Buyer's real problem unsolved
- Competition's primary goal: commissions
- Has poor communication skills
- Causes Buyer frustration
- Disappoints Buyer
- Competition creates difficulties for Buyer
- Doesn't enhance Buyer's image
- Sells inappropriate products or services
- Has poor delivery or service problems
- Has poor follow-up

Selling Move #6

Isolate

An objection is any obstacle that prevents the Buyer from closing with you, that is, giving you a commitment for your product or service. The objection can be about your product or service, your company or even you.

Many wonderful things happen when you Isolate the objection. Isolating means you understand the objection, can explain it in a couple of words with crystalline clarity. You are halfway to a solution once you've isolated the problem.

You isolate the objection by asking questions about it.

When you hear an objection, you may isolate it by asking, *"What causes you to say that?"* or *"Would you please clarify that for me?"* or *"Please expand on that for me."*

When you probe to clarify the objection, half of them go away. They are either answered by Buyers themselves, or the Buyer slides off into a different objection at which point you will have to probe on that one, too. Make sure you understand what the Buyer's words really mean. Any language that uses the same word for love God, love windsurfing, love potato chips, love your child and love your lover is ripe for missed communications.

Well-groomed answers to objections for your product or service can make you a highly paid pro. You should have at least **three prepared answers to every objection** to your business.

When asked, most salespeople say there are limitless numbers of Buyer objections; however, when analyzed, there are only seven objections available to any Buyer. Most businesses we see have only two or three that cost them 80% of their lost sales.

Each objection comes dressed in a number of different, often colorful costumes. Here are some of the disguises:

- **Price**—too expensive, not enough benefits, not worth the money, out of reach of Buyer, competitor is cheaper, wrong price point, etc.

- **Market**—customers won't buy, bad economy, saturated market, not open to buy, competition is better, obsolete design, etc.

- **Terms**—budget won't permit, wrong time of year, poor timing, payment or interest rate too high, etc.

- **Budget**—no budget, not open to buy, bad economy, poor market, too expensive, no money, etc.

- **Won't work**—unqualified [
  has never seen it, heard ab
  wrong product, etc. (see S

- **Reputation**—poor salesp
  employees, poor service,
  specialist, poor sales rec

- **Status Quo**—use comp
  ment, no problem, happy with curr...
  can't see you until later, no need for your service,
  don't understand, call back next week, don't call at
  all, etc.

The Seven Selling Moves

Two Types of Objections

An **Easy Objection** can be answered by your product or service. It's the problem your product or service cures.

For example, let's say that you sell cars. You show the Buyer a blue car.

The Buyer says:

"I like yellow cars."

If you have a yellow car in stock, then the yellow car itself answers this Easy Objection.

An **Inherent Objection** is something intrinsic in your product or service and cannot be separated from it. It

...eature that the Buyer doesn't like or perceives ...weakness. For instance, price is an Inherent ...ction in any product or service purchased. But it ...n be anything: color, your company, your country or even you.

The formula for handling Inherent Objections:

- Isolate the objection
- Minimize the objection
- Offset the objection with Benefits

For instance, here is an Inherent Objection—you have a sales lot full of blue automobiles.

The Buyer says:

"For reasons of love, I drive only yellow cars."

An answer to this Inherent Objection: First, ask questions until you understand the true nature of the objection using phrases like:

"Mr. Krazny, would you explain that for me please?"

"Could you expand on that?"

"Please tell me what you mean."

"Would you clarify that, please?"

Make absolutely sure you clearly understand the Objection. Only then, you can move to the answer itself.

The Buyer then says:

"Well, twenty years ago when I met my wife she was driving a yellow car. We're still married and I still love her vry much. I don't want to change anything that causes me such good luck."

The Seller says:

"Mr. Krazny, I understand your concern about the color (Isolate the objection). *That may not be a serious concern* (Minimize the objection) *when you hear that, because we are overstocked on blue, we are giving you a price of only $100 over dealer cost and one year of free maintenance."* (Offsetting Benefits.)

Isolate the objection to remove the guesswork. As a Buyer, you've seen salespeople answer your objection with a different one you had not considered, and lose the sale with their own objection.

In the Isolation phase, 50% of all objections will be answered by the Buyer. They will simply disappear from the Buyer's mind and never have to be answered. As the Buyer is asked to carefully consider the real objection, another 25% of the Inherent Objections will change into Easy Objections. The message: If you answer the first objection you hear or guess at, you have only a 25% chance of answering the Buyer's true objection. Isolate well and you may never have to answer the objection at all.

Minimizing the objection does not support either the Buyer or the objection. You acknowledge the objection and then put it into the perspective of the whole transaction—small when compared to be big picture. If you support here, you bless the Buyer's objection and are unlikely to close. Then when you try to answer the objection you just blessed, you must reverse your support of the objection. Reversing directions makes you look dishonest. (First you liked it; now you don't.)

Offsetting the Inherent Objection with important Benefits allows the Buyer to look at new Benefits that overbalance the objection. Every sale is a balance between the Seller's Benefits and the Buyer's money. In your mind's eye, see a balance scale. As the sale begins, there is only the Buyer's money stacked on one side that hangs down heavily. During the presentation, you heap Benefits onto your side until the scale tips level; then tips far enough in your favor and the exchange is made. The Buyer owns the Benefits and the Seller owns the money.

Sales are lost over Inherent Objections but not as many as you might think. Most sales are lost because the salesperson has not prepared sufficient offsetting Benefits to answer Inherent Objections. Every product or service has Inherent Objections. The usual response for the ordinary salesperson is to agree with the objection and then discuss the Features (the "F" word).

Inherent Objection examples:

PanDowdy Computer:

Objection:

"We only use Acme Computers."

Answer:

(After probing carefully to understand the true nature of the objection . . .)

"I understand. That may not be an important factor (Minimize the objection) *when you find that PanDowdy has addressed that situation and designed a computer that works in both Acme and PanDowdy environments. Because of the ease of use and compatibility with both systems, you can take advantage of the most efficient products the PC world has to offer and reduce your total costs by 19%."* (Offsetting Benefits.)

or

"That's not a problem (Minimize the Objection).
*PanDowdy has designed computers compatible with Acme
programs which allows you to take advantage of the most
efficient products the PC world has to offer and reduce your
total cost of ownership—hardware, software, training and
operations— by half."* (Offsetting Benefits.)

Rocksolid Malpractice Insurance:

Objection:

"We used you as our insurance carrier five years ago
and cancelled because you weren't responsive in
handling our account."

Answer:

(After probing carefully to understand the true nature
of the objection . . .)

"I understand. You'll find that won't happen again (Minimize the Objection). *We have revamped our entire system
so you can reach one of our agent teams 24 hours a day, 7
days a week to make sure you are fully serviced instantly
making it both convenient and safe for your doctors."*
(Offsetting Benefits.)

Quit selling and solve problems.

Zoom Ball Bearing:

Objection:

"You don't manufacture a full range of ball bearing sizes."

Answer:

(After probing carefully to understand the true nature of the objection . . .)

"I understand your concern. That may not be a critical factor when you take into account that Zoom specializes in manufacturing application-specific bearings that cost 12% less than competitive products (Minimize the Objection). *We will save you time by out-sourcing nonstandard bearings and that 12% you save will contribute directly to your bottom line."* (Offsetting Benefits.)

Pinstripe Management Consulting:

Objection:

"You have no experience with a company like ours."

Answer:

(After probing carefully to understand the true nature of the objection . . .)

"Our experience in your specific industry may not be important (Minimize the Objection) *when you consider*

that we have helped over 150 businesses of all types acquire companies and cut six months off the time to realize profits from the purchase." (Offsetting Benefits.)

Ordinary salespeople feel that every objection must be answered satisfactorily to close. Just the opposite is true. The sale will close with the objections firmly in place if the salesperson has prepared enough offsetting Benefits for the objection.

Are you married? If you are, you know marriage is somewhat less than perfect. Probably knew it going in, right? But you did it anyway. You signed a no-cut contract with a person you barely knew. If you break this contract, it will cost you at least half of everything you make during the run of the contract. Helluva deal. You married because you wanted to in spite of the objections in place. Buyers buy for the same reason, because they want to, in spite of the objections.

Now let's look at Easy Objections. These objections can be answered by your product or service.

The formula for answering Easy Objections:
- Isolate the objection by asking questions about the objection itself until you are sure you understand the true objection

- Answer the objection directly (with your prepared answer)
- Use a Proof Statement if the Buyer doubts your answer

Again, standing in our lot full of blue cars, the Buyer says:

"For reasons of love, I drive only yellow cars."

This time, however, it so happens that you have, in the shop, the most lovely canary-yellow car. This is now an Easy Objection because it can be answered by the yellow car. Isolate first.

The Seller says:

"Would you please explain what you mean?"

The Buyer says:

"Well, twenty years ago when I met my wife she was driving a yellow car. We're still married and I still love her very much. I don't want to change anything that causes me such good luck."

A possible answer to the above objection might be:

"Mr. Krazny, I now understand why you are so discriminating about the color of your automobile. We anticipated

that some folks would prefer yellow, so we special ordered one (Answered directly). *It is being prepared for delivery back in the shop."* (Offered proof.)

Isolating is critical when answering any objection. Isolate by asking flanking probes until you clearly understand the situation. It is important to make sure you know what you are going to talk about. Answering the wrong objection, even well, indicates to the Buyer you have not been listening. When you don't listen, the Buyer defects.

Easy Objection examples:

PanDowdy Computer:

The Buyer says:

"Our company officers are terrified of computers."

You could answer:

(After probing carefully to understand the true nature of the objection . . .)

"I understand. PanDowdy's intuitive operation is so easy the average user can learn how it works and create a usable work product within a half hour. Your officers will gain confidence quickly and enjoy the power and control using their own computer gives them." (Answered directly.)

Rocksolid Malpractice Insurance:

The Buyer says:

"The time and effort we would have to spend changing insurance carriers is just too much for the doctors to bear."

You might answer:

(After probing carefully to understand the true nature of the objection . . .)

"We understand that filling out new forms and medical information gathering can be aggravating for both you and the doctors. We have a staff person that extracts data from your past reports to create a premium quote that requires less than 15 minutes of your time to review and sign." (Answered directly.)

Zoom Ball Bearing:

The Buyer says:

"You don't have marketing experience in Eastern Europe."

You might answer:

(After probing carefully to understand the true nature of the objection . . .)

"I understand your concern. Zoom has partnered with The Zota Corporation, a 50 year-old Paris-based company with

five offices and 80 representatives, to help market your product throughout Europe." (Answered directly and offered proof.)

Pinstripe Management Consulting:

The Buyer might say:

"You are not known for doing this kind of work."

Answer:

(After probing carefully to understand the true nature of the objection . . .)

"We have worked in this field since 1991 (Answered directly). *Two years ago we acquired Realgood Consulting because they specialize in this work and help companies cut merger administration costs as much as 19%."* (Offered proof.)

Examples of answers to Easy Objections from other businesses:

Objection:

"I can't make a payment that size on a monthly basis."

Answer:

(After probing carefully to understand the true nature of the objection . . .)

"We have anticipated that long business cycles might cause difficulty with monthly payments. We can arrange a payment plan to fit your cash flow cycle." (Answered directly.)

Objection:

"I just can't seem to find the clothes I want to carry in large sizes."

Answer:

(After probing carefully to understand the true nature of the objection . . .)

"We understand that and have stocked large sizes in both the sports and dress lines (Answered directly). *We delivered a big order to Empress Sports Wear and they sold out in less than a week."* (Offered proof.)

When you answer objections, don't bury yourself, and the sale, in detail. Like most salespeople, you have worked hard to learn your product or service. Now here is the bad news. Nobody, except you, cares about all that knowledge. Especially the Buyer. This person

---

Selling is a wonderful profession; just don't get caught doing it.

doesn't care about your knowledge. Don't spiral down into the minutia of your own technical expertise. If the Buyer agrees to the Benefits, close the sale and leave. Unless asked directly, don't waste the Buyer's valuable time talking about your extensive knowledge and the nitty-gritty of your business. Buyers don't care. They only care about themselves and their own problems. Keep your information as general as the Buyer will permit.

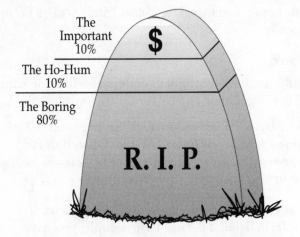

The
Important
10%

$

The Ho-Hum
10%

The Boring
80%

R. I. P.

The Salesperson's Tombstone

Don't bore the Buyer and bury your sale. Stay on top of the information pyramid.

When answering objections, ordinary salespeople overwhelm the Buyer with technical information (Features) that the salesperson is most comfortable with. Then the errors compound.

The Seller goes into a death spiral; they talk too much and vomit their presentation. They forget to sell Benefits thus are on the wrong level of communication, shut down the Buyer's responses, don't support and try to close on yes or no. They crash and another smoking ruin litters the selling landscape.

Selling Move #7

Close

The salesperson's objective is to obtain commitments from the Buyer, commitments that did not exist prior to the salesperson's arrival. Those commitments, at whatever level, are called Closes. The Close is the commitment toward which the other selling moves are directed.

Salespeople make a hobby of designing trick closes. Office comedians always have a favorite story about how a big sale was closed by a clever trick of smart and aggressive salespeople, usually themselves. Like "traveling salesman" jokes, these mini-dramas of persuasion and entrapment make fun story telling. They are trade jokes, however, not professional skills.

Selling is a profession and your income depends on how competent a professional you are. It is an equitable profession. A salesperson making $100,000 a year is exactly twice as good as a salesperson making $50,000 a year. When closing sales, a positive attitude is as important as mechanical skills. However, if you have the mechanical skills, you will soon find the positive attitude to go with it. A fat checking account does great things for attitude.

Trickery in Closing like trickery anywhere else is short-lived.

Ordinary salespeople fear rejection and the close is the most terrifying of all the moves. The Closing probe is used to obtain a commitment from the Buyer. It is also the easiest move to execute if properly prepared. Closing well isn't trickery but the logical outcome of a well prepared dialog. You don't need lots of different Closes, just one that completes the business at hand. It must be simple to execute and memorable under stress.

This is a hard point to grasp, so pay attention.

Use a Closing probe whenever you get agreement from the Buyer.

Read the previous sentence again.

The Close has two parts.

1. First, *assume* the sale is made, that is, the Buyer's problem is solved.

2. Then *ask for the commitment* in the form of technical information required to get your product or service into the actual use of the Buyer. Begin with *who, how, when, where, what.*

This is the textbook structure of a Closing probe. Any idiot can do it. Half the professional salespeople fail to ask for an order at all. Worse still, only 2% of all the salespeople in the country know how to ask correctly.

When you assume the sale is made, several fascinating things happen. When you assume you are there to get a commitment (which you are), you change the way you form sentences and choose words. It simplifies your language. You drop modifiers and conditional phrases such as "If you use our service. . . ." You speak in the present tense. Suddenly, it's "Our service gives you. . . ." This is much more powerful and straightforward.

The successful salesperson operates under a basic assumption that the Buyer has a problem the Seller can solve. Solving the problem today means getting the Buyer's commitment today. If not solved today, it will remain a problem. Your presentation now has a sense of immediacy.

Asking for the order is the simplest move to make if done properly. Many salespeople fade from asking for the commitments because they feel uncomfortable requesting a Buyer to do something for them. More often, they don't know the mechanics of Closing. Ignorance is an uncomfortable place from which to sell.

Closing technically is like eating an elephant—one bite at a time. The Buyer's mind more easily accepts a series of small decisions rather than one large decision.

As a salesperson, you've built a clear and simple presentation and delivered it well. Now, you seem to have some agreement from the Buyer. The problem: how to make the smooth leap from your presentation across your chasm of embarrassment to the Buyer's commitment. It's awkward if you don't know how. It's simple if you do. Use one of the following words to start your Closing question: *who, how, what, when, where.* Finish with technical choices required in getting the product or service into the Buyer's actual use.

Closing probe examples:

PanDowdy Computers:

"When would be the best time to install your new system?"

"How would you like the computers configured?"

"How many stations will you require?"

Rocksolid Malpractice Insurance:

"What coverage plan would best fit your needs?"

"What initiation date would work best for your doctors?"

"How much deductible makes you feel comfortable?"

Zoom Ball Bearing:

"What mix of ball bearings do you feel best fits your needs?"

"When will you determine your annual selling plan?"

"What is the most efficient shipping schedule to your warehouses?"

Pinstripe Management Consulting:

"When would be the best time to meet with the management board?"

"Who will be the point person on this project?"

"What is the due date of our recommendations?"

Simple? No. Ordinary salespeople use Frontal probes — where yes-or-no answers are demanded—as Closing questions. They punch out of the *Soft Sell* at the last moment when it's most critical. They ask:

"Do you want it in red?"

"Do you want it delivered here?"

"Do you want it now?"

"Well, can we do business today?"

And, of course, the auto salesman's favorite selling wreck (with the Buyer's answers in parentheses):

"We want to be your car dealer."
("Who the hell cares what you want?")

"What can we do to earn your business today?"
("How about gettin' outta my face.")

Here is the difference between the old hard-sell close and incremental *Soft Sell* closes.

In the hard sell the Seller dumps a bunch of Features into a hopper, waits for a drop of Buyer's blood to squeeze out the bottom, and tries to close on it with a Frontal probe.

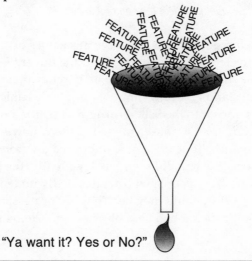

"Ya want it? Yes or No?"

Soft Sell Closes work in a series of incremental and technical bites:

"Who is the point person on this project?"

"When is the best time to get started?"

"What do we have to do first?"

"How would you like the contract to read?"

Most salespeople don't know the mechanics of asking for the order in a way not to offend the Buyer. Fearing rejection, the ordinary salesperson harbors an underlying expectation that a commitment isn't real unless the Buyer jumps into the Seller's arms and plants a big wet kiss. It ain't so. Disabuse yourself of the vain wish that you are due a huge display of unbridled joy from the Buyer because you did your job. Frequently, the best orders are from people who are decidedly undemonstrative. Why should they be? They are professional Buyers. It's their job to be cool. Their egos demand it.

Examples of Incremental Closes from other businesses:

"What conditions would you like to see in the agreement?"

"How are decisions like this made inside your company?"

"How would you prefer to take delivery?"

"What product mix do you feel would work best for your market?"

"What sizes are best for your operations?"

"When would be the best time to begin retraining your experienced salespeople?"

When you are good at selling Benefits and secure at making deals you can graduate to "soft" closes such as:

"Where should we go from here?"

"At this point what would you like to do?"

"What would you like to see happen now?"

"How should we move forward?"

"What are the next steps in this transaction?"

And another approach: Certain people find their closing ratios increase if they suggest a course of action for the Buyer. For example:

"Let's meet Thursday morning at 9 A.M."

or

"For firms your size, we recommend the following product and service mix to maximize your profits."

Closes are much simpler when Sellers remove their egos and rely on the technical information to close the Buyer's commitment for them.

Avoid forced-choice closes: *"Would you like to meet Tuesday or Thursday?"* Everyone knows that hokey old gag; it's the hard sell.

So there you have the Seven Selling Moves. They comprise the skeleton of the *Soft Sell*. In addition, there are a couple of advanced tactical moves that put you ahead of your competitors.

ADDITIONAL TACTICS

The Cross-Sell

Some businesses rely on "add-ons" to survive. Many salespeople need to sell add-on products or services in every interview. Often, the sale of one product or service naturally gives rise to the next. For instance, if you open a checking account at your bank, the natural Cross-Sell would be an overdraft account to keep you out of trouble when cash is short. If you sell commercial real estate services construction management is a natural add-on to asset management. If you sell pie, ice cream is a natural Cross-Sell.

After you have closed your primary sale, you now have a proven buyer. Introduce your Cross-Sell using a 90-Second Close. Salespeople start feeling guilty when they become too successful during a single appointment. Don't get up and leave. Keep selling until you run out of things to sell or the Buyer throws you out of the office.

The 90-Second Close

An advanced move . . .

Here's another efficient and effective tactical move that can be added. Using this tactic can turn you into a world class salesperson who is comfortable in any boardroom.

The 90-Second Close is an advanced selling move that allows the Buyer to make a decision and commit quickly. The Buyer says, *"Hey, I only got five minutes. So make it quick."* You can close in 90 seconds and have three-and-a-half minutes left over to become intimate friends. You can assume the Buyer's problem or need when you only have seconds on the phone, you meet on the street or on a cold call.

Ordinary salespeople do not believe this move works. Field tests show that, if constructed correctly, the 90-Second Close works on large sales as well as small ones. The 90-Second Close was developed for Buyers ready to make a decision and move on without having to listen to a whole sales presentation. It is an excellent way to launch a telephone presentation or a cold call. It is a superb tactic for selling a whole series of products or services in a short time (as in selling a number of items from a sample catalog).

The 90-Second Close is built by joining a Problem/
Solution and a Flanking probe. In summary, you pose
the Buyer's problem, state your solution and ask a
question that encourages the Buyer to answer a logical
question favorable to your cause. When you get that
favorable answer, you Support and Close, asking for the
commitment in the form of technical information
required to get your product or service into the actual
use of the Buyer.

The 90-Second Close structure:

- State the Buyer's *problem or need* (which you either
  assume or determine by probes)

- Offer your *solution or fulfillment* to the Buyer's
  problem or need

- Ask a *Flanking probe* that contains a Closing setup (a
  question that if properly answered, you can then
  support and *close*)

If the Buyer's response is negative, you then probe to
isolate the Buyer's objection, answer the objection, get
agreement and then close. Remember, you are closing
on technical information you need, not the decision to
buy.

90-Second Close examples:

"Mr. Jones, businesses like yours which have thousands of parts in inventory are drowning in numbers but starving for the information they can use for profit." (States the Buyer's problem.)

"Using the Track'em Inventory Software *program and a* PanDowdy *computer you can get the information necessary to detect early trends in the marketplace. That lead time will cut costs for you and can create additional profits of up to 4% annually."* (States your solution.)

"How will a 4% profit on your total inventory impact your annual business plan?" (Probe contains the Closing premise.)

Using a 90-Second Close creates many favorable circumstances in the presentation. First of all, it allows the sale to close without wasting the Buyer's time. It allows the sale to happen so the salesperson can stop on the Buyer's cue; the salesperson can get out of the way of the decision-making; shorten the presentation time; and do something important, like go home and play with the kids. Buyers often become downright resentful if they are forced to listen to you grind out a full presentation. If the benefits up front are compelling enough to close on and the Buyer agrees—close. Give the Buyer a break. Fast Closes make everyone happy.

Some of you say that we aren't talking about your business. Your business takes a full presentation and sometimes many meetings to get the Buyer to commit. The good news is that we *are* talking about your business. Trained salespeople close multimillion dollar real estate transactions in 90 seconds. They allow the commitment to happen and then get on with the job of solving the Buyer's problem. But the problem solving is now housekeeping, the details, the technical side of the business. It's easier to get the commitment first rather than last. The faster the Seller sets up the sale and shuts up, the faster the sale happens.

The 90-Second Close provides a reasonable transition from the previous focus to a new area of attention. Some Sellers have a number of items or services to sell. By using the "Buyer's problem, Seller's solution, Closing setup" format, sequential sales happen quickly. Each setup talks about the Buyer first. If the Buyer knows that the subject under discussion is the Buyer's problems, you'll get their full attention. Ordinary salespeople talk endlessly about their own problems, thinly disguised as a sales presentation.

The 90-Second Close creates the condition to close the sale. There is a selling maxim called "closing from the first word." Ordinary salespeople assume that old adage means to push the Buyer hard. In the *Soft Sell* approach, aggression is submerged. The mechanics of the presentation are constructed in such a way that when the Buyer answers a Flanking probe favorably, the Seller delivers a Supporting Statement and closes technically.

In the earlier example, the Closing setup probe called for the Buyer to work out a scenario: What would he do with additional profit? The Buyer can create a favorable response:

"Well, it could have great impact on our overall profits."

You could then respond:

"You're right. Other businesses have found that higher profits were generated with no increase in sales volume." (Supporting Statement.)

"What approach would work best for you for installing the Track'em Inventory Software Program *and a* PanDowdy *computer?"* (Closing setup.)

Or the Buyer could doubt the figure of 4% increase in profits:

"I seriously doubt that your plan can produce that kind of profit."

By showing doubt, he asks for proof that what you say is true. Delivering the Proof Statement launches you into the very heart of your presentation, which is where you want to go anyway.

Or the Buyer could enjoy the status quo situation and dodge the issue altogether:

"We really aren't interested in computers and software. We are happy with what we have."

When you have a status quo Buyer, you have little choice except to probe for areas of dissatisfaction with a current product, service or situation. A series of Status Quo probes will allow the Buyer to reveal shortcomings of the current activity or reveal their objection to yours. Either way, you are again centered in your presentation.

A properly constructed 90-Second Close is exceedingly powerful. It sets the scene for the presentation, gives you a logical start that is Buyer-oriented and sets up your subsequent moves, depending on the Buyer's response to the Closing setup. Many times it flanks the Buyer's defensive agents.

How do you decide which 90-Second Close to use first? Use background information that you already have about the Buyer. If you have little background, use information gained during your opening probes. In short, the Buyer tells you how to structure the first move to achieve the maximum effect—what that person wants to hear. If you don't have background information to work with, pick your most powerful benefit to sell and structure your 90-Second Close around it.

Prepare a 90-Second Close for every Buyer's problem your product or service solves. The selling power you develop can be surprising. Mastering this tactic allows the Seller to close from any direction on any Benefit or any Buyer's objection. If you can structure a 90-Second Close while presenting "on your feet," you are one of the most skillful salespeople in the country. This skill comes with practice. At some point in your career, you will be paid accordingly.

Example of a 90-Second Close:

"Ms. Smith, your industry is very competitive (Stated Buyer's problem). *National Gadget can furnish you with a competitive edge that can increase your profits as much as 20%* (Stated your solution). *How will a 20% increase in profits affect your stock dividends for this year?"* (Probe containing a Closing setup.)

Other 90-Second Close examples:

Rocksolid Malp ractice Insurance:

" Mr. Jones, from what you tell me, your medical group is suffering because of insurance claims paid where you

didn't feel you were liable (Stated Buyer's problem).
*Rocksolid has an aggressive policy toward claims and
prevents four out of five claims from ever showing on the
record* (Your solution). *What effect would this reduction
in claims have on your doctors' group?"* (Probe containing a Closing setup.)

Zoom Ball Bearing:

*"Ms. Jones, businesses like yours can free up cash by using a
correctly tailored just-in-time inventory program* (Stated
the Buyer's problem). *Zoom has an inventory program
designed to minimize your warehouse time and increase
your ready cash by up to %* (Your solution). *How would
an increase in available cash impact your plans for expansion?"* (Probe containing a Closing setup.)

Pinstripe Management Consulting:

*"Merging two companies so they speak with a single voice is
a time-consuming process* (Stated the Buyer's problem).
Pinstripe *can reduce your merging time by up to 43% and
get your new organization productive sooner* (Your
solution). *How would this decrease in time spent fighting
internal problems impact your managers' morale?"* (Probe
containing a Closing setup.)

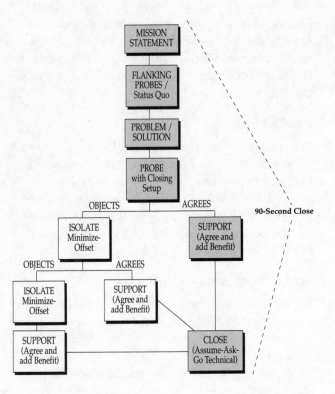

The Tactical Selling Game and the 90-Second Close

13

UNDERSTANDING THE SEVEN MOVES

Fewer disguises than you think . . .

At first blush, it seems that there are countless ways for Buyers to react to a sales presentation. In fact, there is a finite number of responses available.

The Seven Buyer Responses

Greatly simplified, the Buyer Responses are:

1. *"I like what I am doing now"* means **Status Quo.**

2. *"I don't care what you are selling"* means **Indifference.**

3. *"You can't do what you say you can"* means **Doubt.**

4. *"What you say seems reasonable"* means **Acceptance.**

5. *"I don't agree with you"* means **Rejection.**

6. *"There is an inherent fault in your product"* means **Inherent Objection.**

7. *"I don't understand something about your product"* means **Easy Objection.**

The Seven Selling Moves

These Seven Selling Moves are designed to react persuasively to the Seven Buyer Responses. Good salespeople use some of the moves; great salespeople use them all.

And why shouldn't you be prepared? Persuasion is your profession.

You begin your sales presentation with a Mission Statement. If you know the Buyer's problem, you construct a 90-Second Close solution. That sets the scene for one of the Buyer responses outlined above, then:

- If you get acceptance—you support and close

- If you get rejection—probe to isolate

- If you get indifference—probe for areas of dissatisfaction with the current product or service

- If you get status quo—probe for areas of dissatisfaction with the current product or service

- If you get doubt—prove

- If you get an Inherent Objection—handle it as an Inherent Objection (isolate, minimize, offset)

- If you get an Easy Objection—handle it as an Easy Objection (isolate, answer directly, prove if necessary)

In addition to these bare bones moves, use Flanking probes at every civilized opportunity and listen carefully to the answers. When the Buyer says something that helps your cause, Support and include a Benefit. Ignore things said against your cause. When you want the Buyer to express an opinion, use a prepared Flanking *(who, why, when, where, what, how)* probe.

After you have cycled through to answer the Objections and the Buyer agrees with you, Close incrementally by asking for technical information. When you have closed, continue to Cross-Sell additional products and services.

As you prepare your presentation (done correctly this is more properly called a "problem solving dialog") you will notice that of the seven possible Buyer responses, five of them call for a Flanking probe. If you did nothing else except ask intelligent questions, from the Buyer's point of view you would make the right move 71% of the time.

14.

USING THE SEVEN SELLING MOVES

To know and not to do . . .

As a Buyer Response-driven system of communication, the Seven Selling Moves are based on how the Buyer responds. A brief summary of the Buyer's cues and your reaction follows:

Buyer's cue	Seller's move
Acceptance	Closing probe
Favorable comment	Support
Unfavorable comment	Ignore
Doubt	Prove
Status quo	Flanking probe
Indifference	Flanking probe
Rejection	Flanking probe
Inherent Objection	Flanking probe to Isolate/ then minimize and offset
Easy Objection	Flanking probe to Isolate/ answer directly and prove

For new salespeople, it seems that there are countless Buyer Responses and they all mean "No!" Getting people to talk to you can be tough. And when they do talk to you, their messages hide behind their words.

Using Buyer Responses is a shorthand system of selling to reduce the Buyer's thoughts to a single word or two, no matter how confused the response comes out. Buyers are masters of camouflage and confusion. They confuse you and they confuse themselves. Often they don't know what they really think. Your job is to sort out all the pieces, make some sense of it, see the real problems and compel the Buyer to make decisions. It's a paradox. You must assume a leadership role in the transaction while appearing to be a follower. Using this system, you can easily plan a transaction and track it. It's rather simple if taken one step at a time. Remember, these are technical moves, not philosophical statements about life or the ethics of persuasion.

The logic track of the above transaction should be apparent. Selling is a game and the 90-Second Close flowchart shows the moves. Here's the really fun part. Most salespeople don't know about this game. The most common request I get comes late in my sales course— "Please don't teach this game to my competitors." Very often when you play this game, you are the only person in the room who knows what's happening. The power of this game can make you independent of our shaky Social Security system.

Here is a selling scenario. We will play the scene first, then go back and critique it. In this case, we will be selling a product but it could be a service. In a Buyer Response-driven system, it really makes no difference what you are selling. The Seven Selling Moves are the same. In all the scenarios, it is assumed that you have a working knowledge of your product or service and the Buyer is both qualified and the decision-maker. Many times, these assumptions about the Buyer are untrue but more about that later.

You are a salesperson for UP Declavinator Corporation calling on a potential client, a distributor of equipment associated with declavinators. You are meeting him on his turf—his office in the front of a warehouse.

You:

"Mr. Freeman, I'm Cal Kline. I represent UP Declavinator. We deliver upscale products that guarantee a high markup for the retailer and a packaging system designed to make you an additional 4% on each unit."

Freeman:

"Yeah, I've heard of UP Declavinator, but you big guys can't seem to get around to us little people."

You:

"I understand what you mean. UP Declavinator has been selling everything we can produce to the industry giants. Only recently have we been able to expand production to fill the market demand of smaller but very dedicated firms like yours. How is the market compared to what you projected it to be?"

Freeman:

"Actually it seems to be pretty close to our projections."

You:

"That's excellent. You must be doing many things right. Which models move best for you?"

Freeman:

"Our customers demand the medium-duty model. The heavy-duty declavinator buyers live in the southern part of the state. We sell mostly medium-duty declavinators in this area."

You:

"That's smart money. There's big profit potential in medium-duty declavinators. How close are you to your desired markup?"

Freeman:

"Well, declavinators are almost a commodity. It's hard to make a profit on such a commonly used product. Everyone is selling them, 7% is average."

You:

"Obviously you know your market, and finding a medium-duty declavinator that can produce a consistent profit can be tough. UP Declavinator has built in a 10% margin for distributors like yourself. How does a built-in 10% margin work with your overall profit objectives?"

Freeman:

"Well, every little bit helps." (laugh)

You:

(laugh) *"You're right, and keeps you very competitive, too. With your turnover of medium-duty declavinators, we'll package to suit your merchandising style. What packaging will work best for your operation?"*

In response to your introduction and Mission Statement, Freeman disclosed dissatisfaction with your firm. You did not agree with him but showed him you understood his problem. You explained the company's situation in a positive light but implied a Benefit to him.

In testing the water, you asked three Flanking probes about his association with declavinators. Because his responses helped your cause, you supported him each time, making him feel competent. From his information, you designed a 90-Second Close that addressed the medium-duty declavinators, included the problem of profit and solved his problem. When the Buyer agreed, you supported him and asked for the order in the form of customizing the shipment to suit his unique needs.

Too simple, you say. Sales calls never go like that. There is always difficulty.

You're right, they rarely go like that because ordinary salespeople won't allow it to go so easily. Since salespeople know everything about their product or service specialty, their egos compel them to tell everything they know, whether Buyers care or not. Usually, Buyers do not care. If they do, they'll let you know.

But this is just taking orders, you say. No, this is selling—finding the Buyer's needs, filling them, and closing in a timely and workmanlike fashion.

But the Buyer didn't say yes. The order never actually closed, you say. Using the *Soft Sell*, the Buyer won't say yes because Flanking probes ask for a more complex decision than a simple yes or no.

The Buyer will find it easier to agree with you if you are working on technical aspects of the problem rather than working on the way the Buyer makes decisions. If the Buyer answers with information you can use to build a solution, you close technically. At no time will the Buyer say "yes" (or be required to).

Whether there are five or 20 pieces of technical information you must know in order to fill the order, each can be used to close. Even if one of your Closing probes fails, you obtain more usable information each time you ask.

Let's return to our selling presentation. We'll repeat the Closing probe:

You:

> (laugh) *"You're right, and keeps you very competitive, too. With your turnover of medium-duty declavinators, we'll package to suit your merchandising style. What packaging will work best for your operation?"*

Freeman:

> *"Just a minute. What happens if I'm not able to sell your declavinators?"*

You:

> *"What do you mean?"*

Freeman:

"You're trying to stick me with a warehouse full of those things."

You:

"Oh?"

Freeman:

"Well, I know how crazy this market can be. You know I didn't get into this business yesterday. I don't want to get stuck with a bunch of unsold units!"

You:

"I understand your concern. That has been a concern shared by many of our new distributors. We protect you. We will give you a full refund for up to 60 days on any unsold units. That way, you'll have time to get your marketing together and feel secure that we're behind you all the way."

Freeman:

(long pause) "Well, that seems reasonable. I just hate to get hung with stock that I have to sell out below cost."

You:

"You are right. Good businessmen can't make a profit by losing money on unsold stock. UP Declavinator's *guaranteed sell-through program will protect your profits. What color selection do your customers prefer?"*

On your first Closing probe, Freeman didn't close with you but instead, raised an Easy Objection (that is, an objection you could answer directly). Because your Closing probe was rejected by him, it was a *trial Close*. There is no difference between a trial Close and any other. It is only a Close that didn't work. Use incremental Closing probes like you would cook spaghetti; you keep throwing them against the wall one at a time until they stick. Remember to keep them technical.

You answered his Easy Objection by isolating the objection and answering it directly. No proof was required because he didn't doubt your company's policy. When he wanted to tell you he was experienced at his business but couched it negatively, you did not support him but, instead let him know you understood his opinion and that his fears have been shared by his peers. After he considered your guarantee, he accepted your reasoning. You supported him again, gave him a Benefit and moved directly into another Flanking probe calling for a technical decision from Freeman.

A little more like it, you say. Even if Freeman had liked the product from the moment you walked in, there was a good chance he would have made you work a bit before closing. Why? Because he might feel he had not done his bit of bargaining for your time, money or effort. Besides, making the Seller work is the American way. Buyers may make you work hard just to satisfy their own ego needs. Salespeople often take insult from this way of doing business. Don't. It's not personal, only cultural conditioning.

Let's continue with Freeman's answer—he gives you the order:

Freeman:

"Light gray and orange."

You:

"Light gray is an excellent choice. There will be some problem with the orange. We are back ordered several weeks with orange—something about the dyes produced in India are held up in shipping. How about if we substituted another color, say—green?"

Freeman:

"Nope, it's orange or nothing. You people are always playing games with us retailers. Has to be orange."

You:

"Why is orange a requirement?"

Freeman:

"Because I know my market and orange is my big seller. Let me know when you get some orange declavinators; then maybe we can do some business."

You:

"You know, orange may not be important to you when you realize that it may be several months before we can deliver orange. In the meantime, you will lose the profits from those weeks of selling and the potential of losing out to your competitors, too. How will you go about maintaining your competitive position without selling declavinators along with the rest of your related products?"

Freeman:

(pause) *"Well, that's a good point. Competition is tough. I suppose I'd order green if you'll promise me that I'll be the first on the list for the orange when they come in."*

You:

"You are right. Competition is tough. I promise you will be the first on our list for orange when they become available, and that should help you get a leg up on your competitors just as your high season approaches. What mix of sizes do you feel works best for your customers?"

Freeman:

"A gross of size sevens and two gross of size eights."

You:

"That's excellent. Adding on sales can be easy with this product. Market studies show that 25% of your buyers will buy the special declavinator wrench if it's available nearby. How will these painless add-on sales work for your company?"

What happened here? Freeman bought orange declavinators from you that you can't deliver. You did support that part of the Buyer's decision you liked (light gray declavinators), but the rest of his decision was an inherent objection. You answered the objection by making sure you knew what it really was by isolating it, then you minimized it and called the Buyer's attention to potential lost business and the threat from competitors (offset with Benefits). As you isolated the objection, the Buyer quickly reverted to a status quo position. You ignored that response and handled the objection.

The Buyer agreed with your answer but raised an easy objection (i.e., asked for a trade-off you could make). Because you could answer the objection, you supported the Buyer, showed him a benefit to come and closed in the form of his preferred product mix. From this point, you will take the Buyer's order, making sure you have the proper specifications to suit the Buyer's needs. Then, because you have a proven performer, you put forth a compelling reason to buy your add-on product, wrenches, and you opened the new subject with a 90-Second Close.

You ask, how many times do I cycle through and close? As many times as it takes to solve the buyer's problem.

Will the Buyer get tired of me closing? Not if you are closing in the form of technical information rather than asking the Buyer to leap into your arms like a long lost friend. Also, each successive technical Close is based on a successfully answered objection, each having a different Benefit.

If you want to insult the Buyer's intelligence, request an order without giving additional benefits between Closing probes. The ultimate hard close is pounding the Buyer for a yes answer after a no answer has already been given and you have given no additional Benefits to justify changing the Buyer's mind. The Buyer sees yielding to your insistence as a loss of face and confrontational. Save the Buyer's pride. Give the Buyer new Benefits to justify switching from rejection to acceptance.

Learning to apply the proper move to the proper response takes time. This way of thinking evolves with time and practice. Fortunately for us salespeople, there is no special playing field or condition required to practice the selling game. You can play it around the water cooler, at the next board meeting or on your next date.

Unlike the hard sell where the Seller is busy, busy, busy, trying to manipulate the Buyer, the *Soft Sell* allows you to spend much of your time waiting for the Buyer. The meeting moves much slower because the Buyer carries most of the dialog. With well crafted Flanking probes, it takes time for the Buyer to organize and give intelligent answers. With practice, you'll find that your Buyer's responses will be predictable 80% of the time, giving you the opportunity to plan several moves ahead of the Buyer.

With the Buyer doing the talking, you have time to think and respond correctly because of the apparent slowness of the dialog. Learning the *Soft Sell* system gives the you the ability to watch the game in slow motion and set up moves in advance.

Part III

Survival Skills

For The

Street Soldier

15

SELLING BY OBJECTIVE

Picking the goal . . .

Ordinary salespeople arrive in front of the Buyer without a clear objective. Sometimes even experienced salespeople wander into a prospect's presence like chickens pecking though the neighbor's yard—totally without objective except to "see what happens" or "get acquainted" or "introduce themselves." And when the sale doesn't happen, then obviously the prospect "isn't qualified" or "is not ready." So says the salesperson.

Strategically, there are three or four objectives (depending on your type of business) where the Buyer gives you commitments. They are, in sequence:

1. The Appointment.

2. The Contract.

3. The Performance.

4. The Commission.

The Appointment. Many times you can sell your product or service if you can just find the opportunity to tell your story. Since most salespeople are poor at telling their story, nobody wants to listen. The Buyer is asked to commit considerable time and attention and needs a great deal of faith they won't be attacked or bored to death.

The Contract. Sometimes it takes many meetings over several months, or even years, to get to the contract that consummates the sale. The strategic objective never changes. You must have a clear idea why you are in front of the Buyer before you can achieve your objective. (Conceive it, believe it, achieve it.) Unless you can visualize why you are in the appointment and can write it out on the back of your business card in big letters, you aren't going to achieve it without fumbling. When you fumble, it makes you look amateurish no matter what you sell. It's hard to recover your own fumble and score.

The Performance. Many times, getting the Buyer to perform as agreed in the contract means you must keep selling the Buyer into performing the commitment made at the contract stage.

The Commission. In some businesses, such as real estate brokerage and banking, you must sell the Buyer to not only agree to pay you but to actually do so. You not only have to sell your product or service and then keep the Buyer on the contract agreed to, but you must be sure your relatively small share of the transaction is adequately protected so you can buy new shoes for Junior.

Inside these larger objectives, there may be smaller, incremental objectives. Here are some questions to ask yourself to help determine them.

During the Appointment:

- What want or need does the Buyer have for your product or service?

- Can the Buyer's want or need be satisfied by your product or service?

- Is the Buyer qualified to buy what you sell?

- How are decisions made inside the organization? Is the Buyer the decision-maker? If not, who is?

- Are you the logical and most effective supplier for the want or need?

- Will the Buyer commit to using you?

- Where do we go from here? Contract? More information? Another meeting required? See other people?

- How far can you go if the call goes perfectly?

During the Contract:
- Can we sign a contract at this meeting?
- Can we get a verbal commitment?
- Can we shake hands on it?
- What are the terms and conditions of the agreement?
- Are there other conditions?
- Are both parties bound or protected by the agreement?
- Is the agreement enforceable?
- Is your commission or fee protected and collectible?

During the Performance:
- Are both sides performing as agreed? On time? On budget? On specification?

During the Commission:
- Did the Buyer pay as agreed?
- If not, what avenue of collection can you pursue? Collection letter? Legal action? Knives and guns? A big guy in a black suit named Tony the Crusher?

Life and sales go easier when you have a firm grip on where the sale is going and what you are doing in front of the Buyer. Write down your objective each time you call on a Buyer. Keep your objective firmly in mind. Your closing ratio will improve dramatically.

16.

THE COLD CALL

Staying cool in Hell . . .

For some of us, the cold call is condemnation to the eternal hell fires of rejection. Since most of our new business and our new improved commissions are derived from cold calls, we are compelled by the terms of our trade and the demands of competition to get out there and brave the bullets from battered Buyers to bag our brand new BMW.

A cold call isn't as forbidding if you are properly prepared. There are some safe assumptions when making cold calls:

1. Most Buyers' lives will proceed rather successfully if they never meet you.

2. Most Buyers can do very well without your product or service.

3. Most Buyers don't really care to change what they are doing now. It's too much trouble.

4. Nobody cares about the Features of your product or service no matter how new or improved they may be.

5. Unless you can uncover areas of dissatisfaction with what the Buyers are doing now, you don't have a

snowball's chance in hell of surviving the cold call with an order in your hand.

6. Until a series of skillful Status Quo probes proves otherwise, everybody you talk to is both qualified (can use your product or service) and a decision-maker.

You are wasting everybody's time if you can't determine that the Buyer is dissatisfied with current products or services. This is where carefully constructed Status Quo probes are required. They are designed to make the Buyer go inside and develop an answer—the Buyer must stop, think, quantify and make decisions. A probe that gets you a quick answer puts the Buyer on the defensive. Any tip-off that you are selling rather than solving problems will instantly shut down the Buyer.

17

BUILDING A COLD CALL PRESENTATION

A matter of tactics . . .

Take the time to carefully develop six Flanking Status Quo probes for cold calling. Next, develop the possible Buyer's objections (there are only six besides Status Quo, remember?) and answers. Then work up your Supporting Statements and Closing Probes.

The Supporting Statement makes the Buyer feel important or allows you to empathize with the Buyer's situation. The Closing Probe must contain an objective, such as an appointment, and a compelling Benefit that makes the appointment worthwhile for the Buyer. Remember that selling is trading. Trade a Benefit for each thing you want from the Buyer.

Twenty Basic Cold Call Rules

1. Smile, smile, smile. On the phone, your prospect can hear you smile through the telephone wire.

2. Take your time. Relaxation is the first rule of selling.

3. Know your objective and keep it firmly in mind. You can't achieve it if you don't conceive it.

4. Do your homework. If possible, know something about your prospects or their situation. Know your

prospect's business and where they are likely to need help.

5. Use first and last names. Everyone is equal.

6. Don't sound too familiar with new prospects.

7. Use referrals if possible. Mention it twice during the call. Use it only with permission.

8. Being a "silver-tongued" salesperson costs credibility. Don't be too smooth. It makes people suspicious. Some hesitancy is more genuine.

9. Eliminate big words. The more energy the Buyer uses on big words, the less energy available for ideas.

10. Selling is your job. Be good at it. Groom your technical skills like a professional athlete.

11. Don't exaggerate. Use terms of reason rather than hyperbole (i.e., "excellent" rather than "fantastic!").

12. Warm up on unqualified Buyers. Call a few unqualified prospects first to get warm and in the groove.

13. Don't confuse a happy voice with enthusiasm. Use restraint. Sound like a professional. Keep your voice contained and reserved, but not dull.

14. Use your full name and a Mission Statement. Anything else wastes time and makes you sound amateurish.

15. Don't carry the ball. The prospect goes brain-dead when you do.

16. Don't fall into the "Features Only" trap. You have five seconds to get the Buyer's attention. Talk about the Benefits to them personally. The only thing the prospect hears are your Benefits. Apply the Benefits to them.

17. Probing requires great skill. Occasionally Flanking probes may be too difficult or confusing for your prospect. You may have to resort to Frontal probes.

18. Assume the action. When you are closing, assume the sale and tell the prospect what the next course of action will be. In this case, don't ask—tell.

19. Your voice is your tool. Listen to it critically. Is it dull, without life, monochromatic? If it is, practice until your voice has some color.

20. Record—Resolve—Repair. Record your conversations, resolve the problem of where the dialog went wrong and repair it. Then do it over until your presentation works.

Some Practical Ideas

Notes: When working from notes, simplify your list of probes to three and highlight them so you can find them quickly. Also, make the probes as tight and short as possible while keeping them flanking.

Bugs: Bug your phone, record your calls and listen to yourself. Most consumer electronics stores have a simple and inexpensive telephone bug. Attach it to a miniature tape recorder. Troubleshoot your errors and write a script that works for you most of the time. Then stick with it on a word-for-word basis.

Names: If you have a long or difficult name that takes too much time to leave with the secretary, shorten it or change it to a name easily understood, conveyed, and written.

Power: Use simple words and phrases that create simple and powerful images. Look for power phrases and integrate them into your presentation. Beware that they don't sound too corny or dramatic.

Proofs: Present your proofs in dollars or percentages saved or in profits made, if possible. With reputation proofs, use success stories with recognizable industry names to indicate to the Buyer the magnitude of your business. Apply the Benefits of your Proof Statements to the prospect (power, profit, prestige, or pleasure).

Building Your Telephone Tactics:

1. Start with a Mission Statement containing a compelling reason to buy.

2. Then use Status Quo probes and listen to the answers.

3. Answer Buyers' doubt with Proof Statements if required.

4. Close on the meeting by suggesting a specific day and time.

For example, here is a telephone script for getting an appointment with the decision-maker to discuss commercial real estate leases:

1. Set the scene for both you and the Buyer.

2. Deliver a compelling Benefit to the Buyer.

3. Ask a Flanking Status Quo probe to uncover areas of dissatisfaction with what the Buyer is doing now.

4. If the Buyer answers favorably, support the Buyer and close the meeting.

5. If the Buyer answers unfavorably, say, "I understand." Then add the Benefit in dollars or percentages and suggest a time for a short meeting to explain the whole situation.

Seller:

"*Mr. Bosworth, this is Blene Foonman of Acme Real Estate. Because leasing commercial real estate can run into millions of dollars, our goal is to save our clients money by reducing their company's housing costs, often by 20% or more. What have you done to capitalize on the aggressive lease possibilities available in today's market?*"

Buyer:

"*Well, we haven't looked into it at all. We haven't had time.*"

Seller:

(support and close) "*You're right. It is tough to keep up with the market and manage your own business at the same time. When would be the best time next week to sit down for ten minutes and discuss how your profit picture can be improved by taking advantage of this chaotic marketplace?*"

If the Buyer raises an objection, you answer the objection with proof, if required, show how your answer benefits the Buyer, and close again on the meeting. Remember, on a telephone cold call, if you are trying to close a face-to-face meeting, sell the Benefit of the meeting, not your product or service. In this example, don't sell real estate—sell the meeting.

Other examples:

PanDowdy Computers:

Seller:

"*Computer systems are one of the largest overhead costs for your industry. Our goal is to reduce your company's computer downtime by 81%. How have you gone about reducing computer downtime to help increase your peoples' productivity?*"

Buyer:

"*Well I'm not sure what you're talking about.*"

Seller:

"*I understand.* Business Computer Magazine *indicates the computer downtime brings 31,000 businesses to a full stop every month. Let's meet for ten minutes on Thursday morning to see how preventing downtime can increase your company's production and decrease your stress levels.*"

Rocksolid Malpractice Insurance Company:

Seller:

"As you know, good malpractice insurance can greatly impact your medical group's costs and subsequent year-end profits. How have you gone about analyzing the effect malpractice complaints affects have on your doctors' bottom line?"

Buyer:

"We've looked at it but aren't sure exactly how it affects our profits."

Seller:

"I understand. An insurance carrier that doesn't aggressively defend doctors can increase group malpractice insurance costs by 20%. Let's meet for ten minutes on Tuesday morning to discuss how we might be able to reduce your costs and increase your group's income. When would be the best time?"

18.

THE PRICE OBJECTION

Price=Panic . . .

Price always seems to be the most feared objection. For the salesperson, price equals panic. When price becomes the issue nearly every salesperson clutches.

Ordinary salespeople don't believe that what they sell is worth the money; they believe that what they sell is expensive in the Buyer's eyes; they believe that the Buyer purchases on price only and if price isn't the only factor, it is extremely important.

According to Jay Levinson, the guerilla marketeer, price is the fifth consideration to influence Buyers when they make a buying decision. The first consideration is *confidence* (remember, 75% of first-time Buyers bought because they thought the Seller was honest); second is *quality; selection* is third; *service*, fourth, and *price*, fifth. Most Buyers thought price was subordinate to the other considerations. Only 14% considered price first.

In any transaction, assume that the Buyer is going to negotiate price with you. It's the natural thing to do.

Don't bring the price objection in the door with you. Don't mention the price until asked. With enough Benefits, price may not come up as an issue but only as a piece of information.

When price becomes the issue, salespeople get tense. They argue. Or worse, they agree. The Buyer says that price is too high and the Seller agrees. Then to justify the price the Seller starts giving things away—premiums, extra services, the profit in the form of discounts, add-ons, freebies, specials, "value added" features, and anything else the Seller can think of to close the transaction.

Price is an Objection inherent in every purchase. Do ordinary salespeople try to justify the price with the Benefits of the product or service? Rarely. To respond to the price objection:

1. **Isolate the objection.**

   "You seem to have some concern about the price."

2. **Minimize it.**

   "Price may not be your primary consideration when you look at the total picture."

3. **Introduce offsetting Benefits.**

   "Compared to the ability to increase your production by 6%, cut your labor costs by 8% and simplify your management, the return on your investment will repay the modest difference in price twelve times over."

Salespeople die on price because they don't know what offsetting quantifiable Benefits to sell the Buyer.

The fastest way to obtain a second-class price on a first-class product or service is to be unable to explain why it yields first-class Benefits.

The hard lesson about price is that your expertise or products are not enough. You also must pay your own way. You actually buy the business with quantifiable Benefits you bring to the Buyer.

Buyers worry less about the price itself than about how to *justify* the price.

LAW OF PRICE

If you can't explain in words why your stuff is worth your asking price, then it isn't.

Sellers that live with price, die with price. So get your list of offsetting Benefits together (notice I didn't use the "F" word—Features) and when you hear the word "price," you know not to argue about it but to justify the value with the first-class Benefits of your product or service.

19

THE LANGUAGE TRAPS

How to trash yourself . . .

Jargon

Technocrats love jargon. Politicians love jargon. Preachers love jargon. Sales managers love jargon. And of course, salespeople love jargon. It makes us think we sound smart. Jargon is refuge for the insecure.

The only people who don't love jargon are Buyers.

Using jargon on an innocent person is a perfect way to show that you know more about the subject than he does. Yeah. Don't you just love it when a salesperson makes you feel like an ignorant ninny?

The rule: Don't use jargon. Common everyday words deliver your message more clearly. Oh, yes, there are times when there is no substitute for technical terms; but show some discipline, for goodness sake.

Words and phrases that are unclear to a 14-year-old kid are going to be unclear to a qualified adult Buyer. Yes, the Buyer may understand your trick words and phrases, but it takes so much energy to track your idea that jargon hinders—not helps—your cause.

Often Buyers will throw in some jargon to impress the Seller, to show that they are informed. It's a defensive move for the Buyers. It's a trap for the Seller. Make sure your Buyers are as informed as they sound. But be careful. Don't project doubt.

KISS—Keep It Simple, Seller

Simplicity is sophistication. There is no call to use big words. Remember, your idea is your message. Don't trash your idea by trying to impress people with exotic words. Use a simple vocabulary.

Besides, the Buyer forgets 40% of what you say in thirty minutes, 60% in twenty-four hours and 90% in one week. Don't cloak your communication in confusion.

Beware of too much detail. You should know your product or service so well you can explain it clearly in forty words. The Buyer really doesn't care how many degrees you have, just as long as your presentation is easily understood.

Talk Less

Learn to sell in two-sentence bursts; then probe. The Buyer talks 60% of the time, the Seller 40%. Talk more than 40% and you are talking to yourself.

But

When answering objections, don't use the word "but." It indicates to the Buyer that a rebuttal is coming and usually makes you sound adversarial.

Contractions

Don't use contractions to direct a favorable answer from the Buyer. These cheap and transparent tricks offend Buyers. They place the Buyer in a double bind and are best left to pots-and-pans salesmen and other cheap hustlers. The whole premise of selling is to have the Buyer agree with you. How does a Buyer agree with the statement, *"Wouldn't (would not) you love to be the first manager in your industry to install this money-saving software program?"*

The Buyer agrees: *"Yes, I would not love to be the first."* Purge directing contractions like wouldn't, couldn't, oughtn't, mightn't from your presentation. They insult the Buyer's intelligence.

"I Think . . . "

Some reasons not to use "I think . . . "

1. Redundancy. If you say it, you must think it.

2. Pros don't think—pros know.

3. The emphasis is on you rather than the Buyer.

A confused mind always says no.

20

ABOUT MOTIVATION

It's wonderful and it ain't persuasion . . .

Exhortation and motivation go together like pie and ice cream. Salespeople love motivation. It makes them feel good all over. It makes them feel like they can do anything they make up their minds to do. It makes them get up out of that warm bed, dress, squint into the mirror, flash a toothy smile, slap themselves, and say, *"It's show time, folks . . . "* and step out into that wet and gray Monday morning to conquer the world.

That's motivation, a necessity for the professional salesperson. But desire to perform isn't the same as the skill to perform. Skill is mastery of mechanical moves that combine body memory, situation analysis and action. It's the difference between wanting to run and actually running. Or feeling like making love and making love. The hot desire to persuade isn't persuasion. Motivation is emotional; skill is intellectual. Motivation is desire; skill is knowledge.

Salespeople have been carefully persuaded by the business religionists—Zig Ziglar and those other smooth-talking devils—to believe that if you have the desire, you can do anything. True if you have the mechanical skills. Without the mechanical skills, your efforts are love's labors lost.

Motivation is fun to watch and hear. It's great entertainment watching the motivators strut and shout and wave their arms and tell modern fairy tales. They make salespeople believe they are indestructible. They can get salespeople pumping for a while, a few days, a week or even two until they run face-first into the hard realities of the street. Motivation is entertainment, not training.

Desire cannot replace skill. Over time, a skillful salesperson consistently beats the motivated one. As the old saying goes, "Age and chicanery beat youth and enthusiasm every time."

Enthusiasm greatly helps a sales presentation but the more expensive the product or service, the less important the Seller's zeal becomes to the Buyer. A salesperson's enthusiasm for a trick potato peeler can cause a Buyer to go down easily for $1.98. But a salesperson's enthusiasm for a glistening Rolls Royce isn't enough to produce a Buyer's check for $198,000. That takes skill. (By the way, that's a pure Benefit sell.)

In the public mind, sales training is motivation. Many sales managers and business owners feel the same way, so the motivational speech comes during every sales meeting. That's OK. But profits increase if equal time is spent on selling skills—the mechanics.

21

RELATIONSHIP SELLING

When translated, means . . .

Selling is competition. Competition weeds out the weak and allows the public to obtain the best service at the best price. Selling and competition are good for every profession and every business because they are good for the public.

"Relationship selling" is a puff phrase designed by someone who needed to market sales training services to the bankers, doctors and lawyers—all professions philosophically adverse to the concept of selling. Yet each of these professions needs to compete to stay healthy. When big professions don't have to compete they grow great egos that eventually eviscerate the very services the profession was designed to give. Everyone loses. The profession loses its direction and self-respect, and the public loses the best services the profession has to offer.

Relationship selling strives to make the Buyer feel important in the hope that they will overlook other shortcomings you, the Seller, may have. You may not be the best or fastest supplier. You may not have the best product or service. Your professional ego may be way too big. You may not be the smartest person in the world. (Don't worry. There are lots of us not-so-smart people and only one smartest-person-in-the-world. We can beat that person with numbers alone.)

Relying on relationships to sell assumes that everyone's products and services are equal and the only differentiation is whether or not you and the Buyer get along.

Don't rely on relationships to cover up for poor persuasion skills or lack of differentiation of your products and services; the Buyer will deal with a gorilla if it solves the Buyer's problem. Relationship selling also buys into the myth of selling yourself first. Silly.

The ideal customer is a forgiving customer. All salespeople are fallible. We make mistakes. Many times our worst mistakes happen with the clients we need the most. We have to build enough trust so that they forgive us our trespasses. To build trust, you must act in a trustworthy fashion.

The way trust is built:

1. Don't misrepresent what you or your product can do. Tell the truth. In other words—don't puff.

2. Do what you say you will. Or more. Give your clients more than they pay for.

3. Be on time, on budget, and on specification.

The Buyer will deal with a gorilla if it solves the problem.

4. Treat your Buyers as equals—not inferiors, not superiors—and keep them informed.

5. Take an interest in the general welfare of every Buyer. Solve the Buyer's problems even if they're out of your area of expertise. Find an expert in that area and track the results. Your primary interest is your client's success.

6. Represent your Buyer's side of the transaction only.

When I teach banking officers (they talk a lot about relationship selling), they tell me candidly, "Bank customers take a lot of abuse before they leave us." That's a shameful admission, but it's true. We do take a lot of abuse.

When the banking industry got in trouble, bankers got little sympathy from the customers they had abused all these years. The bankers learned what the rest of us know—what goes around comes around. Don't let this happen to you and your profession.

Relationship selling is sublimely logical—treat your clients like honored, wealthy guests that your life depends upon. Because they are and it does.

Here is a test: write down the name of a client with whom you have a relationship. Now, phone them and say these words, "(Insert name of client), I'm a little short this month. Please loan me a thousand bucks for thirty days." If the answer is "Of course," you have a relationship. If he answers anything else, you don't. Period.

On becoming a "Partner" with your Buyer. The word means to share equally in the successes and failures of an enterprise. This is a fraud pregnant with misunderstanding.

If you ask this question of the Buyer, "How do you envision your half of the responsibility in our partnership?" and the answer is, "I will pay your fee," it means that the Buyer isn't really looking for a partner, just a darned good vendor. Be one.

MECHANICS OF EMPATHY

On the right side . . .

We want our friends to empathize with us. Empathy requires certain transactional mechanics. To make friends of Buyers, heed the Dos and Don'ts of the *Soft Sell:*

Do:
- Use Flanking probes
- Listen intently
- Support consistently
- Prove without puffing
- Be Buyer responsive
- Sell Benefits

Don't:
- Vomit your presentation
- Don't guess at the Buyer's problem
- Use contractions to direct
- Use "I think"
- Talk more than 40% of the time

TIME ACCOUNTING

Working for the money . . .

People who sell love self-delusion. Our dream and our natural optimism allows—yes, even encourages us—to plan on getting rich quick.

The hard reality is that most of us get rich hour by hour, day by day, month by month. In the often tedious pursuit of getting rich, some goals need to be established, especially in a profession as uncertain as selling. Here's how to set some goals and time-cost your profession.

Let's assume you work a normal work week but you take two weeks a year off with the family and go to the beach. Your work year has 2,000 hours in it.

Now, write down the amount of money you would like to make over the next 12 months. (Keep in mind that the difference between a wish and a goal is a plan. Your goal should be realistic in that it can be achieved, but will challenge you to do so.)

Annual Income Goal $_____

Now, divide that annual income goal by the number of working hours in one year:

Annual Income Goal $_____ ÷ 2000 = $_____per hour

The result is what you must make every hour of every working day.

To find your weekly goal, multiply the hourly amount by 40:

Hourly $_____ x 40 = $_____ weekly

To find your monthly goal, multiply the weekly amount by 4, or the hourly amount by 160:

Weekly $_____ x 4 = $_____ per month

or

Hourly $_____ x 160 = $_____ per month

So there you have the bare bones of time-costing your trade. But it's a gross figure. Most of us don't sell every minute of every day of every week of every month of every year. We sell in bursts of energy whenever we find someone to sell to. So we must differentiate between the time when we are looking for someone to sell to and the actual face-to-face time of persuasion.

So let's time-cost what you actually get paid for—persuasion time.

Think back over your last five selling days. Calculate carefully, in hours and minutes, the amount of time you spent selling face-to-face. Remember that selling is striving for Buyer commitments that didn't exist prior to your arrival. (If they were service calls, that's just what they were—service.)

Now, divide your weekly income goal by that actual persuasion time for the week.

*Weekly $_____ ÷ _____ hours of actual selling time =
$_____.*

This is your true hourly selling rate.

For most of us the hourly rate is a shocker. Actual persuasion time calculated on an hourly basis often runs $1,000, $3,000, or $5,000 per hour. At these rates, your selling time is competitive with professional athletes, brain surgeons, and personal injury attorneys. Just knowing that actual selling time is the real profit center for the professional salesperson encourages you to learn your profession, to study and demand more discipline of yourself so that when you go to work, you are as ready and steady as a surgeon.

Don't be fooled by all that paperwork back at the office.
Everything except actual persuasion time is overhead
expense. Preparation is required. The more the better—
but it doesn't create cash. Selling creates the fun tickets,
the long green that makes your world go around.

24.

THE DISEASE

From poverty to largesse . . .

Ordinary salespeople work in fear of poverty and dread of scarcity. It's a disease that infects many people and even entire companies. It cramps everyone's style—negatively influencing everything from how a person perceives work to the highest levels of corporate decision-making.

If you work from a center of poverty, cynicism rears its ugly head to protect you from your dread: somehow, someway, the Buyer is going to try to beat you for something—for price, for quantities, for time, for quality—but something.

The rule: A lack of respect for your Buyers only shows a lack of respect for yourself. It doesn't bother them. It kills you.

How can you tell if you or your company works from a center of poverty and scarcity? One symptom is the use of unflattering names for potential customers.

I live in a gorgeous town high up in the Colorado Rockies. People come from all over the world to view the spectacular scenery. And use our indoor plumbing. One winter, we locals, overly prideful of living in a place which others had to travel long distances to visit, hid our sly smiles and superior attitudes toward our visitors and privately we called them names: "See'ers and pee'ers," and "Turkeys" and "Flatlanders." As time passed, not only did our salespeople get cynical, but over the course of a ski season, the whole town turned hard and unforgiving toward our guests, those folks who, in the final analysis, brought the money that kept the town green and allowed us locals to live in that isolated paradise.

Spiritually poverty-stricken management describes Buyers as mooches, lookers, freebies, turkeys, pigeons, marks, suckers, etc. These devices dehumanize the Buyers and allow "us" salespeople to feel superior to "them."

Of course, none of this hurts the prospects. But they can feel when they aren't respected. It hurts the salesperson who must rely on good attitude, good brain-computer input, and good skill. It hurts management because the sales force knows that if management is disrespectful with customers they barely know, how much respect can management have for its salespeople about whom they know everything?

Another rule: The first requirement in the quality arena is an equality between the Buyer and Seller.

If you genuinely do not like the Buyers you sell to, then move into a business where you do. If you don't like Buyers of any kind, move into another business where you can sit alone in a darkened room, crunch a computer, and pick lint out of your navel.

The best friends I have in my life are nearly all prior clients. Many of my future friends will be from the ranks of future customers. In order to be friends, we must be equals. Tacitly, I agree not to demean them if they won't demean me, and then our friendship will be based on mutual respect.

Respect your Buyers and they will grow to respect you both as a professional and as a human being.

25

PERCEIVED VALUE

It's all in the point-of-view . . .

Selling skill and the way you handle the customer are vitally important to the perception your customers have of your business.

According to Tom Peters, 3,000 businesses from all sectors of the economy were divided into those perceived by their customers as better than average and those worse than average. (The operative word here is "perceive," that is, what the customers thought.) Those businesses the customers thought were better than average charged 9% more for their goods, grew twice as fast, increased market share by 6% annually, and averaged 12% return on sales.

Those perceived as worse than average lost 2% market share annually and averaged 1% return on sales.

Obviously quality products and service are important to customers' perceptions. A good image equals even more profits.

A successful salesperson adds quality to the transaction in other ways, for example, by:

- Presenting a good appearance
- Maintaining a pleasant relationship
- Keeping it simple
- Allowing the Buyer to feel important
- Being respectful of time spent together
- Allowing everyone to enjoy the transaction

26

PROFITS IN SOLVING PROBLEMS

Worry about the right thing . . .

If you handle a problem customer properly, you are about to make a friend for life.

Problem customers:

1. Don't complain: 26 of 27 don't report it because they expect no satisfaction.

2. Don't come back: 91% won't come back. (This statistic is the same for expensive and inexpensive items.)

3. Don't shut up: Each complainer tells 9-10 colleagues. 13% tell 20 or more.

Bad news travels fast. And far. (Good news doesn't travel as well— if you do a terrific job, your happy customer will only tell 4 or 5 others.)

Now the good news. 82%-95% become *more loyal* if the problem is handled in a timely and thoughtful fashion *whether or not the problem is solved.*

Put another way, in the big picture, the solution itself makes little difference—the way you handle the complainer makes all the difference. Take care of the customer's feelings well and you own the person for life.

There is a compelling reason why you carefully care for current customers: It costs 500% more to gain a new customer than to maintain a current one.

SELF-TALK

Be nice . . .

When salespeople talk to themselves with their negative inner voice, it whispers things like, "You won't sell this man," or "This woman isn't qualified to buy," or "This company doesn't have a real interest in what I'm selling," or "This buyer doesn't like me," or "I'm never going to close this sale."

As you talk to yourself, those conversations are input into your brain-computer. When you place negative messages there, even casually or humorously, they become part of your thinking process. The subconscious doesn't edit. So when you ask it for decisions made from the input you have given it, the subconscious will deliver up decisions based on the negative information you have placed there yourself.

We all have a recorded tape that plays continuously behind our brain. When it tells us how rotten we are at our job, or at life or love, it's hard to maintain an upbeat attitude.

The rule is: when you talk to yourself, be nice. Don't beat yourself up. Ultimately, you are the only friend you have.

Ordinary salespeople lose sales by talking to themselves negatively.

THE DECISION-MAKER

As elusive as true love . . .

Finding the decision-maker is a universal problem. There is a working method that can help you win more and sell to the wrong person less.

You are with a Buyer and a few Flanking probes into your presentation, you get the sneaky feeling you aren't talking to the person who makes the buying decisions.

The usual Frontal question is *"Are you the decision-maker?"*

The answer demanded by the terms of the question, and the Buyer's ego, is an unqualified yes, whether or not it is the truth.

Forget the Frontal probe. Instead use the following sequence:

"Mr. Jones, how are decisions like this made inside your company?"

If you get an answer like:

"I have to submit it to the board for approval."

You may follow up with:

"When you take a proposal you really believe in to the board, how often do the members refuse your request?"

Usually, you will get an answer like:

"Not very often."

You:

"That's excellent. They must have a great deal of respect for your ability as a manager. Usually, when board presentations go poorly, the presentation fails because the presenter doesn't have enough Proof Statements to back up the request. When you make your request to the board, how comfortable will you feel about the Proof Statements required to make your case?"

If the Buyer hesitates, you can then volunteer:

"Other Buyers have asked me to go to the board with them just to use my technical knowledge as a backup. I will do the same for you with the understanding that I will not sell to the board, just furnish the backup information you request at that time. Otherwise, I won't speak at all."

When you are in the boardroom, usually the second hard question put to your representative creates a touch of apprehension and he or she will cast a worried glance in your direction. You give your Proof Statement. After this happens twice, it becomes obvious to everyone that you should do the presentation. Then do it. Start with a 90-Second Close. The whole thing only takes a couple of minutes and it's happily over for everyone.

If your Buyer says:

   "No. I won't take you to the meeting."

You respond:

   "I understand. Is there anything about this that I haven't made clear that keeps you from standing and defending it during the presentation?"

If the Buyer says no, you can start your close:

   "Excellent. When will you present this to the board?"

The strategy: If you can't close a personal presentation to the board, then close on the Buyer's vote. You may try to anticipate where the Buyer will be weak and actually build a presentation the person can use at the meeting. Simplify your presentation to three points only. Use your strongest Proof Statements and most profitable Benefits to arm the Buyer as best you can.

Sending someone away to do your selling work is frustrating, but life is full of compromise. Do the best you can to prepare them to sell for you.

The mind can adapt to changing conditions but it takes some time to work its way through the old situation and accept a new one, i.e., the loss of a loved one, change of lovers, change of vendors, stopping a bad habit, learning a new sport, or other new conditions. The curve below explains how the mind works to adapt and the mental energy those adaptations entail. If you have any of these feelings as you begin to apply these new skills to your selling life, it is normal. Keep going.

When you take business away from a competitor, remember that in the Buyer's mind, the road to changing important suppliers can be a bumpy ride. You may take some getting used to.

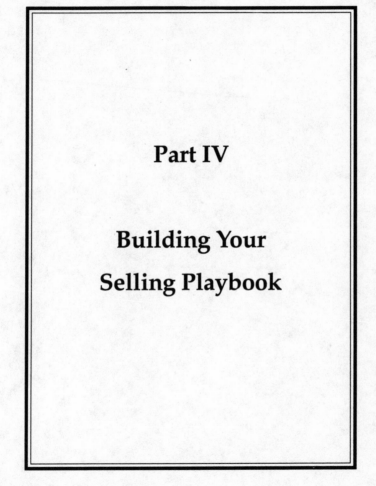

Part IV

Building Your
Selling Playbook

29

BUILDING YOUR SELLING PLAYBOOK

The devil is in the details . . .

Unless you create a Playbook, your personal selling manual, just reading about selling is a waste of energy. You haven't chosen an easy profession so you might as well build a Playbook so you can get good at it. After your Playbook is finished and resides in your briefcase, you'll find it well worth your attention and careful construction.

To build a selling and training manual for yourself and your company, you may use the following format. Your Selling Playbook should be a living document designed to be edited—added to and subtracted from—each time you have a market or business change, have a new marketing promotion and add or subtract products or services. Edit it at least once a month. Use feedback from your actual presentations and revise it until you've built a presentation that works. Test it by reading the changes to co-workers.

The Playbook may be placed in a loose-leaf notebook and tabbed by subject. It should go into your briefcase as standard gear, placed between your sample cata-logue and brochures and this manual. When you are working on the telephone, or in person, you can turn to the proper objection and have several prepared answers. Over time, you will memorize them; but until then, don't "wing it." Winging it is what you do just before your wings fall off and you have a big wreck. Wrecks cost you money. More importantly, they cost time, energy, and attitude—all irreplaceable.

Write your FEATURES AND BENEFITS

Features are for the Seller; Benefits are for the Buyer. The rule: Always sell Features and Benefits together. You may sell Benefits alone. Remember, all we sell is power, profit, prestige, and pleasure, or some permutation of them.

WRITE a list of Features and Benefits for your product or service. Start with your most important Feature and Benefit combination and work to the least important.

       Features   Benefits

Hints:

1. Are your Features important attributes of your product or service?

2. Did you place your most important Feature and Benefit combination first?

3. Do your Benefits reflect power, profit, prestige, pleasure or some permutation of these for the Buyer?

4. If you were the Buyer, would you believe these Benefits if you heard them?

5. Can you prove the Benefits with a Proof Statement of facts, figures or anything else that is quantifiable and real?

6. Did you apply the Benefits to the Buyer personally?

Write your PROOF STATEMENTS

Use Proof Statements when a Buyer doubts your representations. When the Buyer expresses doubt, a Proof Statement calls on the opinion of experts, facts and figures from outside sources, testimonials, industry statistics, or anything else that is quantifiable and real, to establish credibility with the Buyer. It removes puffery from your presentation and makes your presentation sound real.

Key features of the Proof Statement:

- State the Benefit you are going to prove for the Buyer
- Prove the Benefit for the Buyer using facts, figures, etc.
- Apply the Benefit to the Buyer

Write six Proof Statements about your product or service. Use your most convincing Proof Statement first.

Hints:

1. Do your Proof Statements quote credible, believable sources?

2. Are they convincing?

3. If you were the Buyer, would you believe them?

4. Do your Proof Statements discuss Benefits for the Buyer rather than Features?

5. Do they apply the Benefit directly to the Buyer?

6. Do they discuss the opinions of you or your company? (They shouldn't.)

Write your MISSION STATEMENT

Use the Mission Statement as an introduction to the Buyer. To build a powerful and profitable introduction, it should contain a compelling reason to buy from you, and the central theme, most important benefit or a snapshot of your business for the Buyer. If you already know your Buyer, use it to set the scene for the presentation.

Tell your story in 40 words or less. Include your name, why you're taking up the Buyer's time, what kinds of problems you solve, and the Benefits of your solution.

WRITE three Mission Statements for your product, service, company, or yourself.

Hints:

1. Does your Mission Statement state your personal or firm name?

2. Does it state the Buyer's problem or need in general terms or by implication?

3. Does it state your solution to the Buyer's problem or need?

4. Does it then give the Buyer Benefits of your solution?

5. Does it contain a compelling reason to deal with you?

6. Can you read it aloud three times easily? If you can't, keep editing it until you can.

Write your SUPPORTING STATEMENTS

Identify opportunities to support the Buyer. Using the Buyer's words, WRITE six statements made about you, your product or service or about the Buyer that cry out for your Supporting Statement. If it's a status quo Buyer, any dissatisfaction with the status quo can be supported.

Use a Supporting Statement whenever the Buyer says something that helps your cause. It makes the Buyer and you feel good. This is the most effective and eco-nomical selling tool. Remember to agree with the Buyer and give a Benefit (not a Feature) of your service.

Be careful not to support Buyer statements that go against your cause. Ignore the negative remark and respond with a Flanking probe to find out why.

WRITE a Supporting Statement for each of the Buyer's favorable statements given above. Remember, first you agree with the Buyer with "You're right . . . " or an equivalent. Then add a Benefit of your product or service.

Hints:

1. Does your agreement keep the center of effort on the Buyer ("You're right..." as opposed to "I agree...")?

2. Does your statement take the global view, that is, compliment the Buyer personally on his or her grasp of the big picture?

3. Does each statement include a different Benefit of your product or service?

Write your FLANKING STANDARD PROBES

Standard probes are questions you'll ask during every new meeting that obtain information you need to qualify the Buyer and get acquainted. They should flank the Buyer's armor, that is, make the Buyer stop, think, quantify, and make decisions. They should not imply the Buyer's poor judgment in the past, present, or future.

WRITE six Flanking Standard probes.

Hints:

1. How much information does this question demand from a new Buyer?

2. Is it tactful?

3. Does the question leave the hint that the Buyer has made poor decisions in the past or present, or may in the future? (It shouldn't.)

4. Does it make the Buyer stop, think, quantify, and make decisions?

5. Does it start with how, who, when, what, or where?

6. Can the Buyer answer by merely saying yes or no? (They won't be able to if the probe is well-constructed.)

Write your BEST OF ALL POSSIBLE WORLDS PROBES

These probes allow the Buyer to dream of an ideal situation or design the perfect transaction from their point of view. WRITE three.

Hints:

1. Does your question set up the Buyer's imagination without the usual constraints of reality?

2. Is the question posed without connotation, limitation or constraint?

3. Is the question self-serving for the Seller? (It shouldn't be.)

4. Does the question expand the Buyer's view rather than limit it?

Write your EMERGENCY PROBES

These probes are to be used whenever you are pressed, stressed, lost or confused. WRITE two.

Hints:

1. Does your Emergency probe place the ball in the Buyer's court?

2. Does it sound intelligent?

3. Does it buy you time? Will it take a few seconds for the Buyer to formulate a reasonable answer?

Write your FLANKING STATUS QUO PROBES

The Status Quo probe is designed to uncover the Buyer's dissatisfaction with the current products or services. It can't attack the Buyer's decision-making, but it can (by implication) show deficiencies in your competitor's products or services. Or it can raise needs that the Buyer has not considered before.

WRITE six Flanking Status Quo probes.

Hints:

1. Is your Status Quo question Flanking?

2. Does it begin with who, how, what, when, or where?

3. Does it try to reveal weaknesses or shortcomings of the Buyer's current product or service without attacking the Buyer's judgment in the past, present, or future?

4. Is it likely to uncover hidden needs or dissatisfactions you can sell into?

5. Does it mention your competition by name? (It shouldn't.)

Write your PROBLEM/SOLUTIONS

The Problem/Solution reveals your solution to the Buyer's problem or need. It is not an introduction.

After you have determined the Buyer's problem or need with Flanking probes, state your Problem/Solution.

Prepare a Problem/Solution for each Buyer's need your product or service fills. Since what we all sell is power, profit, prestige, pleasure, or some permutation thereof, any Feature you discuss must include one of these important Benefits your product or service delivers.

The Problem/Solution should be 25-35 words long, must state the Buyer's problem or need first, then state your solution or fulfillment of that need. Ideally, your solution should also contain the company or service name.

Key features of the Problem/Solution:

- 25-35 words.
- Buyer's problem given along with the Benefits of your solution.
- Your solution includes firm or product name.

WRITE a Problem/Solution for each problem you solve
for the Buyer.

Hints:

1. Does it contain 25-35 words?

2. Does it state the Buyer's problem or need first?

3. What is your solution to the Buyer's problem?

4. Does it include your company or product name?

5. Does it include an important Benefit?

Write your OBJECTIONS AND ANSWERS

An objection is any obstacle that keeps the Buyer from closing with you. Well-organized salespeople prepare at least three answers, including a Proof Statement, to each Buyer's objection.

Write your Buyer's objections starting with the toughest ones, those that cost you the most business. Of the seven objections, most businesses have only three or four that really lose most of the business. Usually price is one of them.

WRITE seven of your company's most expensive objections expressed in the Buyer's words:

Now, make the decision: In each case, is it an Inherent Objection or an Easy Objection?

INHERENT OBJECTION: something intrinsic in your service; it can be a Feature that the Buyer doesn't like or perceives to be a weakness. In handling Inherent Objections:

1. Isolate the objection.

2. Minimize the objection.

3. Offset the objection with Benefits.

To get a good start, WRITE a list of the Benefits you offer your Buyer that offset the price objection. Justify your price with Benefits (not Features) that you offer.

Write your OFFSETTING BENEFITS

EASY OBJECTIONS are those that can be answered by, or problems solved with, your product or service.

In handling Easy Objections:

1. Isolate the objection.

2. Answer directly.

3. Offer proof if necessary.

ANSWER THE OBJECTIONS.

Now WRITE three answers (or just one if you want to get started quickly) to each Easy and Inherent Objection you hear from your Buyers. Include proof.

Hints:

1. Does your answer first Isolate the objection so that you understand the problem clearly?

2. If it's an Inherent Objection, does it minimize the objection?

3. Does it use your product or service benefits to offset the objection?

4. If it's an Easy Objection, does it answer the objection directly?

5. Does it prove the answer with something quantifiable and real?

6. Are your answers forty words or less? (Fewer words are preferable.)

7. Is your answer clear, unequivocal, and without puffery?

8. Is your answer convincing?

9. Are you sure this isn't a Status Quo objection which should be handled with Status Quo probes?

In your answers to your Buyer's objections, WRITE in the name of each part of your answer thus:

(Question carefully to make sure you understand the objection . . . Isolate.)

"I understand that it is important for your to have a vendor who can work with our people in Dallas as well as those here in New York (Answer directly). *We have an office in Dallas."* (Offer Proof.)

Write your INCREMENTAL CLOSES.

The Close obtains a commitment from the Buyer that didn't exist prior to your arrival. Use it whenever you get agreement from the Buyer. That agreement can be subtle—a dropping of the eyelids, the opening of protected body language, a simple nod of the head.

The Close has three parts:

1. Assume the sale is made.

2. Ask for the order in the form of technical information required to get your product or service into the actual use of the Buyer.

3. Begin the question with who, how, what, when, or where.

Since a *Soft Sell* Close requires that you ask technical questions requiring answers to get your product or service into the actual use of the Buyer, WRITE five or more Closing Probes that you'll ask the Buyer.

Hints:

1. Does your Closing Probe begin with who, how, what, when, or where?

2. Does the question require technical information required to get your product or service into the actual use of the Buyer?

3. Does your Closing Probe imply bad decisions by the Buyer in the past, present or future? (It shouldn't.)

4. Do your Closing Probes ask for only pieces of the Buyer's commitment rather than a total commitment in one big bite? (It should.)

Write your CROSS-SELL

Once you have closed, your Buyer is now a proven performer. Many businesses create substantial additional profits by selling additional products or services.

WRITE your Cross-Sell opportunities below

First, Close on: then, Cross-Sell:

Write your 90-SECOND CLOSE

This advanced move combines a powerful Problem/ Solution with a powerful Flanking probe which if correctly answered, allows you to close. Use it to close at the top of your presentation or when time is short.

The 90-Second Close should be 25-35 words in length (not including the probe). It must state the Buyer's problem or need first, then state your solution or fulfillment of that need. This move should end with a probe containing a Closing setup that if properly answered, allows you to support the Buyer and start closing.

The 90-Second Close:

1. 25-35 words (not including the probe).

2. Buyer's problem given along with your solution and the Benefits. Include a compelling reason to buy.

3. Probe contains a Closing setup. (If correctly answered, you can close a piecet of the Buyer's commitment.)

Write a 90-Second Close for each Buyer's need. Since what we sell is power, profit, prestige, pleasure, or some permutation thereof, the Feature you discuss must also include an important Benefit. It works best if the Benefit is a compelling reason to buy.

WRITE at least five 90-Second Closes for your business.

Hints:

1. Does your 90-Second Close state the Buyer's problem or need first?

2. Do you then offer a solution or fulfillment of the problem or need?

3. Does your benefit contain a compelling reason to buy?

4. Does it end with a Flanking probe that contains a Closing premise?

5. If the question is favorably answered by the Buyer, what Supporting Statement will you use (in actual words)?

6. If the question is favorably answered by the Buyer, and you support well, what words are you going to use to start closing the transaction?

30

PREPARE A TACTICAL SELLING PRESENTATION

From the sidewalk up . . .

When prepping a sales call, many top salespeople work up a customer information and background sheet—name, address, title, company name, etc. You'll also find it profitable to include a tactical selling plan that includes the following:

- The objective (the Appointment, Contract, Performance, Commission) should be spelled out clearly.

- The Mission Statement you will use

- The Status Quo probes you will use

- The Buyer's problem or need you will most likely uncover

- The solution you will furnish the Buyer

- The Benefits of the solution you will sell, including Proof Statements

- The Objections you will most likely hear

- The Answers to those objections, including Proof Statements

- The Closes you will most likely use

Lastly, add a section for the follow-up information to make sure the Buyer gets the full service you promised during the sales presentation.

Skill can save you when luck runs out.

31.

PRACTICE

On the playing field . . .

You can't become a world-class salesperson without practice. Lots of practice. Fortunately, if you are a professional salesperson, you have a fertile field in which to practice your *Soft Selling* skills.

The more you practice, the better you get, the more sensitive to the Buyer you become and the more money you make. It's that simple.

The suggested practice plan goes like this: actively study and practice 20 minutes a day for three weeks. (It takes three weeks for new knowledge to become integrated into your presentation.)

After that, study and practice for 30 minutes twice a week. Don't get lazy or forgetful with your practice times. Pick one *Soft Selling* move each day to concentrate on. Make that move every chance you get. Soon you'll watch your presentation change right in front of your eyes.

Don't underestimate the value of constant practice. One student of the *Soft Sell* practiced every morning for years. Five years after he took the course, he telephoned me to say that he had just made three presentations and created $1 million. He now owns a big piece of a warm skyscraper in the heart of the cold, cold city.

Okay, I know this is an extreme example. But where the payoff is potentially huge, isn't practice worth the effort?

When you leave a presentation, troubleshoot it. Determine where it went wrong—where you made mistakes—and correct them. Take the time and your skills will improve dramatically.

The bottom line: Hard practice yields great skills which deliver great money.

Practice, practice, practice. It's only your profession.

32.

POSTSCRIPT

This little book isn't everything you need to know about selling. Persuasion at the professional level takes ambition, study, awareness, creativity, a touch of luck, and a bunch of skill. We have discussed skill only because there is so little written about transactional skills that persuade the Buyer to commit. It is the most difficult because it is the only piece of persuasion that is quantifiable in dollars and cents.

You may have one final residual suspicion after reading this. "If this Vass guy is so smart, why ain't he rich?"

Well, I am.

I work when and where and with whom I like. I live with a woman whom I both respect and adore, have more projects on the drawing board than I can ever produce, travel whenever I like, maintain terrific clients and have wonderful friends. I turn down work when I feel like it. I love my life.

I was born a blue-collar baby. None of my good life could have been possible without living in the USA.

But every country gives each of us, to some degree or another, opportunity to change our lives and improve our lot. The real truth is that not everyone can be president or prime minister. Some of us have been dealt weak hands. But there is nothing in any country that says we can't improve our hand with study and work. And that's the glory of persuasion—the opportunity to improve our hand.

I have been sublimely lucky. America, business, and life have been good to me.

I pray your country, your business, and your life's work will be good to you, too.

Jerry Vass
Telluride, Colorado USA
1998

ACKNOWLEDGMENTS

Thanks to Jan Miller who patiently listened to so many half-assed ideas; to Howard Camber who always challenges what purports to be conventional wisdom; to Roy Musgrove who inspires me to stay tough; to Tazewell Vass who finally discovered the adventures of entrepreneurship; to Rachel Vass, my alter ego and production guru who suffers through, and eventually saves me, in every project like this book.

Thanks to Greg Jones, my editor who cut the words without carving up the ideas.

And a special thanks to Iris Herrin, my fearless helpmate in business and in life who laughs at my jokes, lends her talent, argues persuasively, tolerates my insanities and always encourages me to leap into the fearsome abyss of untested ideas.

All teachers stand on the shoulders of those that taught before, brave souls that shouted down the tunnel of darkness and heard no echo and went on teaching anyway. I learned from them that, with or without reward, one has to plunge on through the fog, do honest work, and hope for the best.

For me, after much arm waving, ranting and shouting into the darkness, the best of echos has finally come back.

Those dedicated teachers, some I knew and some I didn't, made my terrific life possible.

J.V.

Goodman, Gary, **Reach Out and Sell Someone, Break-throughs in Telemarketing,** and several others, Prentice Hall Press, New York.

> This author publishes a series of books on telemarketing. Much of what he teaches fits the *Soft Selling* format. I recommend his stuff.

Lanham, Richard A., **Revising Business Prose**, Second Edition, Macmillan Publishing Company, New York, 1987.

> I recommend this wonderful little book to my students. It teaches an infinitely valuable tool for salespeople — clear thinking.

Levinson, Jay Conrad, **Guerrilla Marketing Attack,** Houghton Mifflin Company, 1989.

> Levinson seems to have a real-life approach to selling — something rarely seen in the book world — and good ideas for small business.

Peters, Tom, **Thriving on Chaos** , Alfred A. Knopf, New York, 1987.

> While his books are too fat for busy people (and skinny books don't demand fat prices) he has good figures and good stories.

Turn your car into a classroom

Soft Selling in a Hard World, the audio tape. Unabridged, read by the author. Four cassettes in album; 3.5 hours. Turn off that rock 'n roll and turn on your sales.

When VASS Becomes a Verb

Vass Executive Sales Training Workshops. Three day courses that teach hard-core mechanics that often return 500% to 1000% on tuition costs.

A Gift For Your Friends

Soft Selling in a Hard World, the book. Page 166 alone is worth the price.

Our Guarantee

Everything is guaranteed, of course.
Like you, we must perform or die.

Call **1-800-424-VASS** (8277) orders or information.

EXECUTIVE SALES TRAINING
www.vass.com